RECKONING WITH OUR AFRICAN ANCESTORS

Hey Auntie
Please accept this token —
of my Love; You are true family

Michele 4/6/07

fool huh!

RECKONING WITH OUR AFRICAN ANCESTORS

Reclamation and Atonement by
Their Descendants

Michele L. Albert

iUniverse, Inc.
New York Lincoln Shanghai

RECKONING WITH OUR AFRICAN ANCESTORS
Reclamation and Atonement by Their Descendants

iUniverse books may be ordered through booksellers or by contacting:

iUniverse
2021 Pine Lake Road, Suite 100
Lincoln, NE 68512
www.iuniverse.com
1-800-Authors (1-800-288-4677)

Library of Congress No. TXu1-318-090

ISBN: 978-0-595-42279-1 (pbk)
ISBN: 978-0-595-86616-8 (ebk)

Printed in the United States of America

THIS BOOK IS DEDICATED TO THE STRENGTH I'VE RECEIVED FROM OLODUMARE (GOD) THE CREATOR; AND THE GREAT SPIRITS ORUNMILA, ESU, OBATALA, OSHUN AND ALL OTHER BENEVOLANT ORISHAS. AND TO THE MEMORIES OF OUR AFRICAN EGUNGUN (ANCESTORS); THAT DEMANDED THIS WORK BE WRITTEN; AND TO MY RELATIONS; MILDRED, KEITH, MARSHA, LOLA AND KYLLE FOR THEIR LOVE AND SUPPORT, M. TOUSSAINT, MARQESHA J., A. MARISSANTE FOR THEIR WISDOM, QUESTIONS AND PATIENCE I LOVE YOU TOO. BABA O. OGUNSEYE AND APETTEBI IBEYEMI OGUNSEYE, FOR THEIR STEADY SPIRITUAL GUIDANCE AND MY GODCHILDREN THAT INSPIRE CREATIVITY, AND RESOLUTION.

ABO RU   ABO YE   ABO SI SE
(May Sacrifice be accepted)
(May Sacrifice preserve life)
(May Sacrifice Manifest)

CONTENTS

INTRODUCTION

HOW AND WHY THIS BOOK WAS WRITTEN IS TO FOLLOW; WHEN YOU BEGIN TO HONOR YOUR ANCESTORS (EVEN IF YOU DON'T KNOW THEIR NAMES) VERY INTERESTING THINGS START TO HAPPEN (like family will call or have a picture of your great grandfather to give you or you will get list of names of people that you never met, but they are related), THEY RESPOND TO YOUR PRAYERS. THEY RESPOND WITH URGENCY, THEY WANT TO ADD TO YOUR VOICE, AND ARE GLAD WHEN YOU CALL. WE ASK QUESTIONS BUT DON'T WAIT FOR THE ANSWERS. ON THE DAY THE ANSWERS COME, DON'T ACT SUPRISED. THIS WORK IS FOR, AND, BY OUR COLLECTIVE ANCESTORS (EGUNGUN), THEY WOULD NOT LET ME SLEEP OR REST UNTIL THIS WORK WAS COMPLETE.

I TRIED TO STAY TRUE TO THE FLAVOR AND INTENSITY THAT I FELT DURING THIS PROCESS. SOUNDS A LITTLE LIKE CHANNELING EXCEPT WHEN IT'S YOUR PEOPLE (They really don't take no or any excuse!), BECAUSE IT'S REALLY PART OF OUR SUBCONSCIOUS.

LET THIS BE AN INFORMATION GUIDE FOR YOU ON YOUR JOURNEY OF RECKONING, IT WILL BE ALITTLE PAINFUL BECAUSE WE MISS THOSE WE LOVE. I GUARANTEE IT IS WORTH THE DISCOMFORT AND SLEEPLESSNESS.

THANK YOU!!! MAY OLODUMARE BLESS YOU!!!

'THE PRIVILEGE IS OURS TO SHARE IN THE LOVING'

ALMIGHTY GOD, OUR HEAVENLY FATHER, THE
PRIVILEGE IS OURS TO SHARE IN THE
LOVING, HEALING, RECONCILING MISSION OF YOUR
SON JESUS CHRIST, OUR LORD, IN THIS
AGE AND WHEREVER WE ARE. SINCE
WITHOUT YOU WE CAN DO NO GOOD THING.
  MAY YOUR SPIRIT MAKE US WISE?
  MAY YOUR SPIRIT GUIDE US?
  MAY YOUR SPIRIT RENEW US?
  MAY YOUR SPIRIT STRENGTHEN US?
SO THAT WE WILL BE;
STRONG IN FAITH,
DISCERNING IN PROCLAMATION,
COURAGEOUS IN WITNESS,
PERSISTENT IN GOOD DEEDS
THIS WE ASK THROUGH THE NAME OF THE FATHER
      CHURCH OF THE PROVINCE OF THE WEST INDIES

'LIFT EVERY VOICE AND SING'

Lift every voice and sing
Till Earth and Heaven ring
Ring with the harmonies of Liberty;
Let our rejoicing rise,
High as the list'ning skies let it resound loud as the rolling sea
Sing a Song full of faith that the dark past has taught us,
Sing a song full of the hope that the present has brought us;
Facing the rising sun of our new day begun,
Let us march on till Victory is Won.

Stony the road we trod,
Bitter the chast'ning rod,
Felt in the day that hope unborn had died;
Yet with a steady beat,
Have not our weary feet,
Come to the place on which our fathers sighed?
We have come over a way that with tears has been watered,
We have come, treading our path through the blood of the slaughtered,
Out from the gloomy past, till now we stand at last,
Where the white gleam of our star is cast
God of our weary years,
God of our silent tears,
Thou who has brought us thus far on the way;
Thou who has by thy might,
Led us into the light,

Keep us forever in the path, we pray
Lest our feet stray from the places, our God, where we met thee,
Least our hearts, drunk with the wine of the world, we forget thee,
Shadowed beneath the hand,
May we forever stand?
Tru to our God,
Tru to our native land

By James Weldon Johnson 6/17/1871–6/26/1938 A book called Negro Americans, What Now?, calling for civil rights; his brother composed the music J. Rosamond Johnson. This work is known as the Black National Anthem, and we are proud of this work.

DESTINY AND SPIRITUALITY

I have grown up in a very Spiritual family as most Blacks in America, who practiced the Baptist doctrine, and, as many African children in the Diaspora do; we have questions which never get answered, about faith, family, God, Why, why, why? And Yes!!! I asked all those uncomfortable questions of anyone that would listen, the Ministers, Deacons, Deaconesses, Elders and Parents: Why would God allow slavery and misery for Black people? Is there reincarnation? How do we know? Why doesn't the Church help more poor people? Why do we spend so much time talking about each other? How can you be really good all the time when some get away with being so bad? What are we doing here and how do we find out? Questions from children seem never to be important or get answered and so they are constantly seeking. Now I understand that they asked the same questions when they were young and did not get an answer either.

Firstly, I was Baptist (the preachers kids were rotten that's standard isn't it!), then on to Islam (too much spying on the single sisters, I was always in hot water), then nothing (still believed in God but I was not going to another, make you feel guilty for being alive Church), I studied Catholicism (I was very interested in the Saints and their Powers and Dominions), and Buddhism (there was no place for the Black people as a culture and heart was not in talking someone into a different belief structure, because I believed in compatibility of faiths); a serious seeker. I soon realized they were excellent attempts at formalizing religious doctrines and dogma; however they all seem to raise more intense questions than answers. Again, Catholicism; Christianity were used by our hijackers to keep us as physical, mental and spiritual prisoners, and I wondered what part did those other beliefs play in our traitorous capture?. Black Africans realizing this fact would bring positive changes to all aspects of our lives at this time by revamping our systems to include new information that has become valid in this century, and coming to some kind of conscientious achievement. The total Black population probably would take about 50 years, at least a generation to shake off the mind numbing dogmas wouldn't the freedom and power (ASE) be worth it. I couldn't see how our circumstances were going to improve for the better; it felt like our hands were tied. Unless by some miracle, we <u>all</u> become; Priest and Priestess and multi-millionaires (with a different understanding of what wealth is and how to use it); regaining our freedom, pride, humanity, ethics, values and morality at the same time, but that would be just too difficult for some to undertake. Big Miracle! Next and LAST, I've been studying Ifa for years and dreaming of my Ancestors; and it has culminated in several years of interesting self discovery and the word novice still applies. Ancestors reveal in your dreams too!

Ifa (the system of divination from Orunmila, who gave human being the ability to physically communicate through Odu Ifa with Spirit (Orisha), Ancestors (Egungun) and OLODUMARE [God]); the system that gives answers, remedies and solutions for our life situations; Ifa is not a stagnant cultural system, because after your first divination and you complete the prescribed actions; the next time you have one (divination) it will address a different part of your condition. I highly recommend Black African Human Beings in America read a few recommended works found in this work, and see if you feel a familiarity through Ancestor DNA/RNA. Cellular memory will seem to come alive for you; maybe an epiphany, an amen, an I heard that or an Ase. Our Ancestors have been unyielding they are not at all happy with the state of our people. We were brought here in chains, now being able to vote, quite an accomplishment on so many levels.

An Odu Ifa is the circumstance that surrounds you or the situation that you're trying to understand; here we find the remedies. One; Odu Ifa (out of 256 possible combinations), I will share at this time, after several attempts to find the Odu that pleased the Ancestors and kept me very restless all last night and well into the following day, finally; Ancestors had me to look up not just any Odu to illustrate their point; but one having to do with dishonesty. "The Odu Ifa; is Ogbe SA: Ifa says that no matter the condition in which this client may find himself or herself, he or she must never lie. He or she must never cheat or be dishonest. Ifa says that those who are cheating the client will find themselves to blame in the end. The affiliated (want to speak), Heavenly Spirits and Orisha of this Odu Ifa, Ogbe SA; are Ifa; Esu Odara (Ifas' messenger); Ori (clients guardian or head); Ibeji (twins, multiple births, two ways of seeing same thing); Osun (medicine, protection); Egungun (Ancestral spirits); Orisha-nla (Obatala, creation, wisdom and purity). A few forbidden (taboos) for Ogbe SA are: Must never lie or be dishonest; Must not eat maize(corn); Must not eat pounded yam; Must not use or play with palm-fronds; Must not use Agbigbo (bird of vulture family) for any purpose; Must not engage in fasting; Must avoid stubbornness, stupidity, carelessness and ignorance; Must not go out without informing his/her household about his/her whereabouts; Must not go out at night or be attending night parties frequently. Ogbe OSA children must beware of friends. They must not be revealing their whereabouts to their friends. They must not follow any friend to anywhere without informing other people where they are going and the people they are following. These are necessary in order to prevent being kidnapped or abducted by those he considered to be his friends. Must speak the Truth" There could be any number of reasons Ancestors chose this Odu Ifa; my guess is that I am always contemplating ways to wake us up at the same time, wake us to what?, our word is not our bond anymore, trust is gone, the work is not done, we have a hard time trusting ourselves, let a lone others. The remedies for our solution are in this Odu. Not everything but a start. The others are studying our spirituality and practicing our cultural traditions without good character, or a clue."

This Odu Ifa was taken in part from:

Practical Ifa Divination by S. Solagbade Popoola pg 296 Yoruba Theological Archministry, Brooklyn, NY

It is a great comfort, in being Soul satisfied; on a physical and mental level that invisible yet constant pressure is eased. Ifa divinations provide sound reflections and should be performed by a practicing Babalawo, Priest or Priestess, before any major decisions or undertakings are made to ensure that you maximize the opportunity for success in your lives, and with the recommendation of the Baba or Priest (ess), there may be a need for regular reading until you have a handle on things and can track your progress or healing in life. You will get a better knowledge and insight of your pathway, destiny and spiritual path. There are many stories (Odu Ifa) that offer remedies to our problems and answers to many of our questions. Also with that understanding there comes' fewer deadly conflicts, but just like anything if you aren't ready to hear what is being said, your struggle may be with your ego. Ifa brings peace and harmony within; you begin to recognize that people you encounter as having a sacred head (Ori) also, Ancestors as well. Oh that do unto others … seems to fit here. This is of paramount interest for us to see and experience the connections (following your taboos will keep you out of most messes). This is only the beginning to getting our true spirituality and culture back, how many pieces of the puzzle are out there, that have been lost and stolen due to the deterioration of our culture? THEN WE CAN HELP OTHERS; US FIRST!

Epiphany!!! We must understand that there are no accidents we seek silently or in prayer, and if we are paying attention, the answers come. While in this perpetually seeking mode I was introduced to a few people (that were also seeking), that eventually lead to a Master Teacher called a Babalawo (Priest of Priest). A Babalawo is a Priest of Orunmila and the keeper of the Spirituality, Traditions, Knowledge and Culture our people; and a Priest of Orunmila. He is the major conduit, emissary and clarifier of Odu Ifa. He literally walks between worlds, they are no joke. What is said in a divination should be written down so you can follow those instructions, because the Baba may be speaking for an Orisha or Egungun (Ancestor) and this information is vital to your healing.

Ifa has been practiced for thousands of thousand of years before Christianity or anything else. It is considered the first spiritual practice of civilized human beings based in Truth (Live and let live; Help don't hurt). Just think Ifa had to be reconstructed and reintroduced herein the Americas; does that amaze you, it amazed me that it to survive; it revealed to me how extraordinary we truly are. I also discovered that Ifa was the unifying spirituality used by the African elders and Obas (Kings) of various nations, to figure out what mistakes we made to end up in these conditions.

To unify the African nations enslaved here in America, the Elders and Priest Council needed to seek the Truth of it and get some direction and answers; paramount was to recreate the much needed humanity, values, spirituality, morality, and a strong sense of community, we abandoned to survive during slavery. This powerful practice of Ifa was the unifying way of life and spiritual strength encompassed by all Africans in one form or another in this Diasporas; fortunately we had to drag our sacred with us because we became too comfortable and complacent, when you take things for granted you eventually loose your center, and soon nothing is worth your time, so we have become the Slave trade. It (Ifa), worked then to make us remember who we were, and to remind us what greed will do, and to know what lack of good character will provide us; and, Why Not give it a chance to teach us those lessons that are much too painful for us to think about, Now?

Believe me I am a novice in the vast understanding that I am trying to explain it takes a life time or two, but when a people are on the brink of destruction something has to work that has been neglected and over-looked.

"Knowing many things, does not constitute having knowledge. Even having knowledge of ten thousand assorted pieces of information does not constitute having understanding. Knowledge or understanding does not mean you have the Truth."

By Honorable Conrad E. Mauge PhD

Earlier I mentioned that the Elders, Babalawos and Priest were forced into slavery and were responsible for masterfully disguising our Orisha (Essences of God), Deities and Rituals into the dominant religion of this new land, ensuring that our essences wouldn't be lost. Now we must capture that lost information in the form of bones, artifacts, scrolls, etc. from whom; you guessed it! Egungun (Ancestors); want us to rethink the relationships we have with each other, and roles they play in family. Before it's too late!

The survival of Ancient Egyptian Deities, through Yoruba Orisha; camouflaged in Christianity are touched on in the chart below. Aren't we clever!!!

EGYPTIAN	YORUBA	CHRISTIANITY	GR/ROMAN	TAROT
Bast/Du	Olodumare	God	Zeus	Wheel of Fortune
Horumla	Orunmila	Jesus	Apollo	Temperance
Khnum	Obatala	St. Jude	Eos	Emperor
OT	Yemoja	Virgin of Order	Poseidon	Empress
Set/Keeper	Elegba	St. Anthony	Hermes	Magician
Khu	Ogun	St. Peter	Mars/Ares	Chariot
Shu/de-lo	Ochossi	St. Norbert	Pan/Diana	Judgment
Ba-lufon/Nef	Oya	St. Joan of Arc	Aeolus	the Tower
Ra	Shango	St. Barbara	Helios/Dionysius	Justice
Kh-onsu	Oshun	Virgin Mary	Aphrodite	the Star
Pua-nit	Babaluaiye	St. Lazarus	Hecate	the Hermit
Khu	Iku	Becoming Spirit	Fates	Death
Neter/Nut	Ifa	Bible	Runes	Tarot
Nefer	Ile	Sacred Place	Rhea	Earth
Osiris	Orisha Oko	Abraham	Cronus	Sun
Orion	Oro	Voice/Prayer	OOOO	Hanged Man
Khu/bon	Egungun	Ancestors	OOOO	the Moon
Geb	Gelede	Eternity	Ambrose	Strength
La & Da	Ibeji	Good & Evil	Amphion/Zethus	Lovers
Amon	Oni/Babalawo	Pope	Baptist	Hierophant
Hor	Ori	Cardinal	Sibylla	the World

Millions of enslaved Africans were from western regions of Africa so even though they spoke in various tongues there was a unified respect for the elements (environment), region, and cultural differences; and one of the major cultural and spiritual beliefs (that Survived) Ifa. Ifa philosophy is a sophisticated wisdom which reflects the customs, value, way of life and morals of our peoples and their descendants. (See; Ancestor memory)

In Ile Ife (Cradle of Yoruba Culture), Ifa is a precise system which permeates every aspect of daily life; for believers or non believers. Divinations are performed as often as your life needs, or to foresee any upcoming events that may need caution and clarity, or how to enhance or lessen the impact of positive or negative events to your advantage through proper reverence and offerings. This ensures harmony within the community; imagine everyone operating on the same page and taking an active responsible part in the health and well being of the entire community. You still have free will and you can choose to participate by doing your part; because this same community will assist you when in need. Wishful thinking, we have become so far removed from who we are suppose to be that our cellular memory and skin color is all we have to remind us and preserve our wisdom, there is so much corruption and greed leaking into the world that it seems as though everyone is one kind of slave or another. Like Now!!!

Another important part of Ifa Divination and Spirituality is the Naming Ceremony, because rather you are fortunate enough to have parents that will guide you or not what is revealed about you in this Ceremony is significant to you, I discuss this Ceremony later. The Ceremony usually occurs within a matter of days after the birth of a new member of the community family. During this Ceremony the Babalawo calls upon Olodumare; the Ancestral Spirits of both parents and the Guardian Angel (Ori), that accompanied the child to Earth. What you will discover is not only the life's' destiny of the child, but also which side of the family tree this spirit has returned from (Reincarnation).

Marital status, Wealth, Longevity, Fertility, Enemies and Prosperity questions can be answered by consulting a Babalawo; who can give you the prescription from spirit, to overcome those obstacles and problems currently in our lives, by reading the Ifa Odu during divination. What a feeling of hopefulness and control; being awe struck by living your life according to what Olodumare (God) decree, and you find out that you asked the gatekeeper for, right then, and right now. We are the inheritors of the Spirituality of our Ancestors. It's very liberating to realize why we are here, 1-burden lifted; time saved in your pursuit of a professional career, guidance is identified for you, 2-burden lifted; what kind of spouse would best fit into your life plan, 3-burden lifted, will you be blessed with children, and so on. What will and won't work for your life's destiny. Understand that is if you seriously want your life and the lives of your family to be better in the long run.

There are a lot of paths to take, but look at what's working for us. Do you have a better idea?

When operating in the system of Ifa you can readily see the common threads that bind the various religions of today and where they got their information. It's not a difficult stretch to understand the persons purporting to be the masters, having their need to be placed first (God complex), in the minds of the enslaved congregations; to maintain control, using brutality, fear, and, murderous tactics so where has that arrogance got them or us, WAR. Because of our potential unifying belief in Olodumare (God); the masters needed to replace the concept of our God with them. OOOH fed that Ego. We must remove our own shackles in order to bring civility back into the realm of the living; otherwise we are destine to repeat and repeat this oppression; our descendants will not have access to this information due to the fact it is being changed while we sleep, history is being rewritten and we are written out (we were happy to work like beast of burden-BS and expected to work for free), or why we did what we did, stop doing the only manual jobs we could get because too many of us lost our lives, and buried under most buildings and bridges.

The other remarkable revelation concerning Ifa is that it is all inclusive, in our lives naturally; not dogmatic, like do anything wrong and go to hell, or there is no redemption for the hand you were dealt. Our Ancestors were brilliant. What, we need is an explanation that makes sense in our lives! We are our Ancestors (they are us, we are them); we have a destiny to fulfill in America. Therefore we all have a similar fate or destiny. Freeing ourselves from believing the negative press and negative portrayals of us in this society and around the world will show us how to free the rest, understanding who we are and how we are being manipulated should give us insight to be responsible for ourselves and others; if you are tuned in you will not have to run into the streets to get recognized (they would just put us in some concentration camp). Ifa divination was given graciously to us by Orunmila; to communicate with Olodumare, Orisha and Egungun (Ancestors); to positively maneuver through our daily lives, staying on our paths to enrich generations and our families. What a revelation for Us First then the World; "When the sleeper awakens …" Dune the Movie

These sixteen Truths of Ifa were presented by a Baba; "… used as the very first step in acknowledging that there are powers greater than man …" C.E. Mauge The Yoruba World of Good and Evil

This list was compiled by C. E. Mauge after many years of research.

1. There is a single God.
2. There is no Devil.
3. Except for the day you were born and the day you are supposed to die, there is no single event in your life that can not be forecast and, when necessary, changed.
4. It is your birthright to be happy, successful and fulfilled.
5. You should grow and obtain wisdom during this process.
6. You are reborn through your blood relatives.
7. Heaven is "home" and Earth "the marketplace". We are in constant passage between the two.
8. You are part of the Universe in a literal, not figurative way.
9. You must never initiate harm to another human being.
10. You must never harm the Universe of which you are part.
11. Your Temporal and Spiritual capacities must work together.
12. You are born with a specific path. It is your goal to travel it.
Divination provides your road map.
13. Our Ancestors exist and must be honored.

14. Sacrifice guarantees success.
15. The Orisha live within us.
16. You need have no fear.

The Yoruba World of Good and Evil C.E. Mauge

The Universal Truths are within the Ifa Creeds, which can be found in various camouflaged forms in religions of today; with many esoteric changes. In most cases they were meant to be self serving; (i.e. Bible; King James Version purported to have been written by Shakespeare). To keep us off balance, Jesus had hair like sheep not hair like corn silk, and confused about the truth and what we believed in.

Stop denying that the extripation of Blacks never happened or that we need to get over it or that we are doing so well or those Blacks that fall through the cracks are just ineffectual. If we pull our heads out of our arrogant behinds then reconciling with our Egungun (Ancestors), maybe we can really start to get over it. I want some help because I really don't have answers, except a couple ha; unified belief and an instant boycott of any thing that offends anyone of us.

The following; Oni bode (is a term in Yoruba that basically means Gate Keeper): Is the Ifa truths; how we decide to come into this world. And why we do have control over our situations and with proper sacrifice, humility and good character, we can lessen those problems we continually encounter, for ourselves, our families and our African countrymen. No matter how devastating the situations may become or has been our Ancestors left us the tools to rectify our position. Divination is most helpful tool in discovering answers to our questions, problems, circumstances and desires. Remember while Europe was in their Dark Ages; our African Civilizations were in their third Golden Age, check out any Museum (Smithsonian).

ONI BODE
('THE GATE-KEEPER')

Onibode: Where are you going?

    Person: I am going into the World.

    Onibode: What are you going to do?

    Person: I am going to be born to a man named $\underline{X}$, of a woman named $\underline{Y}$, in the town of $\underline{Z}$. I shall be an only son. I shall grow up to be handsome and in favor with everybody; everything I touch will prosper; when I am Twenty-five, my father will die and when I am Fifty, my mother will die. I shall build a large house and possess a large prosperous farm; and be the father of a large family through my twenty wives. When I am Sixty years old, two of my children will have a quarrel and one will be killed. At the age of Ninety, I shall be ill for a short while and then die peacefully in my house, to be mourned by all; and to be accorded a grand burial.

    Onibode: To!!! (It is sealed).

(Olodumare God in Yoruba Belief by E. Bolaji Idowu pg. 184)

This conversation with the Oni Bode (Gate keeper) happens for each of us when you are petitioning to be reincarnated, therefore when our lives don't seem to take the path we think, and then an adjustment needs to take place; an affirmation can take place with a divination. Your Ori (head-destiny) offers to accompany you on your path to guide you in fulfilling the destiny you asked for, and to learn the lessons that life has to teach you. Mostly we feel that we have the power to achieve our aspirations without help from anything, wrong! The sooner we figure it out the better!

All of this and more can be revealed with a periodic divination and during a naming ceremony (Esentaye, third day ceremony) for a new born. This is when the parents find out how to best spiritually raise and guide their child's life, what the taboos (things that are forbidden) may be; what professions best suits them, and what kinds of things should be avoided from business contracts to spouses. However when you are older and are seeking to make since out of the hell your in, you discover religion again or some form of it. You should go for a reading (divination) and it is revealed that you are in the wrong occupation or all those abortions you had were actual gifts from Olodumare (God), and sometimes you requested certain things from the gate keeper (Oni Bode), or how important you are to the World and so on. Divinations are prescriptions for your life, to get you back on track; so if you have one please do what the hell the diviner (a repeatable one) tells you it is for you and only you to heed.

This original rendition of the Creation story I felt was important to include, basically because another perspective on who we are and what we believe stems far beyond our understanding of what we have been told these days. Rather you believe my understanding of the facts or not; rather you change your religious doctrine or not is not my goal; it is to put information on the table, which I felt was important for us to lay hold of, because I cannot say we are GREAT enough!

CREATORS' CREATION

"Tradition teaches that at one time the Earth was a watery marshy waste-land that was visited from time to time by the Orisha for the purpose of hunting. Idowu says that they descended by strands of spider's web which also formed bridges by which they walked over the marsh.

Olodumare decided to create the World and entrusted Obatala with its' creation and provided him with a snail shell full of earth, a five-toed hen, and a pigeon. Obatala descended on a chain, chose a spot, and dumped out the snail shell full of earth, forming the first mound. He then let loose the hen and pigeon and they began to spread and scatter the earth until a large expanse of the marsh was covered. Obatalas' servant Agemo, the Chameleon, because of his extraordinarily careful and delicate way of walking and ability to look in two directions at the same time, was sent to inspect the work. On his second visit he reported that the earth was wide enough and dries enough for habitation. This first sacred mound of earth was called ILE-IFE; The House Widening. This name speaks of Ife as the place where the 'Yoruba' first perceived of themselves as being distinct from their neighbors and having a common family Ancestry. It also marks

Ife as the home of original dispersion for all migrating family branches no matter how far flung. This story also tells us that at some time in the primordial past the area in question was a marshy tract that was only visited by Ancient Heroes for the purpose of hunting and that these Heroes constructed what could be considered the forerunners of the hunters perch, Egu."

(Orin Orisa songs for selected Heads by John Mason; pg 73)
Yoruba Theological Archministry, Brooklyn, NY

REALITY'S ILLUSION

With your Roots implanted
Determined not to Move
There is a bigger Demon
That has outfitted us with wooden shoes
My Soul is Healthy and Strong,
Though I am bruised
From Birth wedded to Spirituality,
My Determination will long
Given the body of a Warrior, the Mind
Of a King
And the Force of many Tribes
Being Lord's of our own rings
Freedom we seek, peace we bring
Savoring the last few ounces of Liberty
In my canteen
To quench this thirst during my last quest
Will fortify my Family to Preserve Life's Breath

—Lateef Lucas & Marcellus Brown©2004

PRAYING, MEDITATIONS AND SPIRITUAL EMPOWERMENT OR MESSAGES AND DREAMS FROM EGUNGUN (ANCESTORS)

In 1993, I proudly went through an ancient African ritual passed down from our Yoruba Ancestors. Many rituals have been reinvented and reworked in the Diasporas (the act of dispersing; to spread; to cause to vanish). Because we long ago lost the ability to foresee and fulfill our cultural and spiritual voids produced by extreme oppression, as well as the need for formal rites of passages, in the Americas. Ancestors knew we would need to stay connected to survive. This powerful ritual spiritually re-connected and formally bonds me with my Egungun spirits; whether I knew their names or not. As a result I have felt quite transformed and relieved to know that I can work to positively elevate (spiritually and karmic) the direction of my whole family each day for the better, and lessen the guilty feeling that we are not doing enough to preserve our heritage, so little by little bit by bit one by one we will be victorious.

Please understand I am not trying to paint rainbows, but I can not watch and listen to the same old platitudes spewing out of the mouths of people that just don't get it.

Even if we have difficulty communicating with each other or we are on opposite sides of the country, I can take the issue(s) to our Egungun and trust that it will be handled in a protective, loving and kind way, on their time schedule. We need to reckon and ask for protection for all Blacks with Iwa Pele (good character), and guess what? You don't have to know their names; just do it.

I have witnessed many situations that needed fixing, such as driving while black or traveling to a new city and the police don't know you and the questions fly or wholesale murder by police of blacks and blacks being murdered by the medical professions and institutions, I have prayed about it because things in our environment will kill you with out blinking, that prompted me to march, protest, write, call, testify or what ever I could to protect my family, relatives, friends, god children and anyone that I could help, those of you that haven't lost the gifts; know what I mean. So later when I get a call saying I'm fine, we arrived safely and all is well I like many mothers thank Olodumare (God). With that kind of focus expect remarkable results.

As you will see I have been asking questions, fighting, reading and getting misunderstood since day one, so if you need to take a few months to read this work I truly understand.

Being concerned about everything harmful that might or has happened to my family members, friends and the rest of us on a daily basis is not acceptable, but who do I think I am? I am revolutionary, an activist, mother, women, friend, grandmother, godmother, healer, spiritualist, wise women, mentor, medical professional, teacher, counselor, disaster volunteer, businesswomen and much more. These things that I am, I'm proud to be, so that determines what is highlighted during my daily prayers and paying homage and reverence to Orisha (Spiritual aspects of God) and Egungun helps me to make clear my actions for the day; who do I need to see, call or avoid. State the concerns you have with faith and your expectation that the problem will be resolved, to the best interest of our families and the person (s) involved. Most important don't have a negative hidden agenda or it will kick you in the ass (just a side bar; not my issue anymore☺). Because as a young head strong person, I would wish disease and plagues on my enemies, just like everyone else. I quickly found out that this kind of negativity has to go some where, it stuck to me.

Consider taking these prayers and meditations one step further; to include extended family and the African Community World Wide. With these Ancestor reverences a new freedom comes from being empowered to protect and assist our people. Imagine the positive impact and effect on their lives and yours (we could use the dates of Kwanzaa as a collective prayer experience) to elevate and unify, not to control. Unity is not a unique experience or concept for other cultures that are just arriving, but we, Black African people can use some practice (any faith) and, give an African focal point and support to uniting our families' lives. We as a collective have to do something to combat this constant assault on us or we will be extinct (gone, not here, was). They do it!

Do what! Have a collective focus that is only about our success and growth.

Imagine the collective group of us in the Diaspora (dispersion), not being able to communicate with each other (due in part to Willie Lynch), because of the centuries of distrust, so in spite of Willie we choose a day to put our prayers together for our causes and elevation. This would let our Ancestors know we are unified for the New Year and we respect ourselves and each other. This will have an empowering affect on all of us.

Our African culture must be redesigned by resetting our priorities to insure we do not become extinct. Remember who we are and what we have accomplished in the past. We had a great history before slavery! We continue to have many defining accomplishments to our credit to this day. We know how to turn a cow's ear into a silk purse, so let us do it for ourselves.

Because, we as Black Africans need to be concerned about our spiritual health and preservation, which should be the PARAMOUNT duty of us all, RIGHT NOW, (not however at the destruction of any others but for our restoration). OUR ANCESTORS DIDN'T GO THROUGH HELL FOR US TO FORGET, SQUANDER, DISCOUNT, AND IGNORE WHO WE WERE AND CAN BE AGAIN.

Africans seem to have forgotten that our initial contact with God; gave us the first glimpse into our pivotal position in the universality of existence (the bringers of civilization and humanity). These fools will parish if we become extinct, there is a balance after all have you heard any music without bass, it sucks. Notices how the weather has changed for the worse, storms have become destroyers and the Earth seems very upset that so many of us are being killed at the hands of a jealous enemy.

However for the past 404 years we have been in a constant state of war, fighting to preserve our lives, family, spirituality, community and culture; but the last 600 years seems as if we all have developed a brain freeze. It's like we forget who the enemies were (the devils) and what they are capable of. Now is the time for us to create new frames of reference (Black African ones). "SANKOFA" is the remembering what and who we left behind, "go back and fetch it". All peoples follow their origins; now Black Africans must follow their origins and celebrate where we have come from: Africa. Egungun say we should be most concerned about our future, as spiritual, cultural, moral, trustworthy, whole, and honest, human beings, the basics. Save our families, children, and heritage. This is a War, for the SOULS of a mighty people!

Per Mr. J. Smalls, "the five most basic concerns of African people right now are food, clothing, shelter, meaningful vocations, safety and security", until we have become spiritually and culturally aware these are the main life sustaining things that we all absolutely need, or think we have covered. But we are always seeking to obtain the bare essentials that we could lose at any minute. Mr. James Smalls also gave important definitions to a few words we use, and have no idea that we are not analyzing but perpetuating the misinformation from the HIJACKING: "Economics—is actually the manipulation of commodity and how that impacts the sciences and Ecology. Politics—is the sociology of our Ecology and the management system of our Economy. Culture—is the Psychology of a society and determines whose interest is represented in the Economy and Politics."

This is why Ancestor worships and reverences are of utmost importance; culture is the most spiritual connection we can share with each other, "it's an African thang".

The best of the knowledge repository is our Ancestors; their concepts, and how we process information, and ideas were truly within our culture, and we have the only keys to revive and save ourselves.

By creating new frames of reference we can begin the process of removing those shackles from all aspects of our lives and STOP perpetuating the beliefs, teachings and the lies we have been told and taught. We did not flee Africa to come here at any cost! This means we have the same experience that can be a spring board to developing a strong cultural healing.

DREAMS AND CORROBORATION WHY EGUNGUN WORSHIP IS SO DAMN IMPORTANT FOR BLACK AFRICANS

Egungun= (Ancestor) worship is to REMBEBER, and Connect with the Wisdom, Values, Power, Strategies, and Spirit; of the all encompassing knowledge of our blood relatives, that have passed away; but still check in with us, IBA BA T' ORUN=Homage to Generations in Heaven. The healthy Melanin energy that is our gift and essence is also what connects us directly to Olodumare (God). This linkage is possible and imperative for all Africans, we need to take seriously; others have, i.e. melatonin pills, tanning pills; were do you think they got the melanin to study? How do you make orange juice from an orange? Our gifts include the interpretation of events, with our vibration that cannot be matched; we are the glue that holds this planet in 3rd position, to know our importance in the scheme of things is vital. They just woke up one day and Pluto is not a planet WHAT THE HELL, the day is coming when they will say Blacks are _____ gone.

Understanding Ancestor (Egungun), worship is a powerful tool for us to use and healing families and the planet; to have a gigantic positive that we control; reconnection with our Loved Ones that preceded us and chose to educate us in the process. We aren't here by accident; we have been recycled to get it right. There is a bigger job than only recovering from this hijacking and enslavement or just to survive, didn't we do that. If and when we combine our wisdom, dreams, souls, experiences, discipline and energy; we will figure out how to close the Ozone hole and recover extinct species, get our priorities together and be economically strong.

Our Egungun (Ancestors) had adamant (unyielding) spirits to survive and recreate them in us. We need to recapture this indispensable trait, not just to elevate ourselves but all of the others as well. FIRST THINGS FIRST!!!

The ritual of contacting and honoring our Egungun (Ancestors) allows us to diminish the hate, guilt, grief and pain of their choices; as well as giving them loving messages. Updating the Egungun on their family situations since their departure (is pretty much for our benefit). Egungun pretty much knows what their bloodline is up to. Just imagine how healing this can be for those left with the burden of painful memories and questions of why?

Abusive relatives that have now become Egungun (Ancestors), depend heavily on your forgiveness; because they remain in the do not recycle bin, when you have a divination you'll find that out. Those that had bad character can be respectfully told, about the absolute hell they put you through. They need forgiveness and you need to forgive your self. Or so and so, is incarcerated, you ask that they please protect him/her while there and get them out a.s.a.p.; or so and so, might be on drugs (Rx/Designer) and you need the assistance of the Egungun to impact the situation, for the benefit of that family member. They can also guide you to the love of your life; of course along with Olodumare. Just Ask!!! Another very important aspect of Egungun worship is you must make good on any promises you made to that family member because they DO NOT FORGET; no matter how tough or how long its been, they can make your life hell. KEEP THE PROMISES OR DON'T MAKE ANY. This is very important when healing a family of its secrets and other stuff. If for example you are having difficulty conceiving it may be an Ancestor in your way, doctors can't fix that!

If you still aren't sure, consider the value of Egungun worship in your life and consider your family members and their current circumstances; even if you don't speak to each other. That relationship can and must be healed. Some times if they did you wrong Egungun will make them take care of you even if they hate your guts; NO LIE. <u>EXAMPLE:</u> An Elder, is very ill; and if you are performing Egungun worship regularly; you may let the Egungun know that a descendant may be crossing over soon and you are encouraging them to be present; and you want them to petition Olodumare for the Elders healing and for their life; do not be too sad if they pass, because you know the spiritual work has been done, it just may be their time. Or a child has been kidnapped and you need them (Egungun) to relay an escape plan and/or facilitate the Childs safe return, and to apprehend the sick scum that made the biggest mistake of their lives. Or when you were young you had an abortion and are ashamed to talk about it, and now you realize that all pregnancies are Ancestors and gifts, you must respect. These are ways you can feel you're in the game and doing something useful, not sitting on the side lines helplessly watching the incompetent be, more incompetent where we are concerned. This is one reason I have fought to keep clinics out of High Schools, they have a statistical agenda to keep track of us and make sure we get abortions without the knowledge of the parents.

What this does for you is develop a positive atmosphere in your environment for the healing and/or crossing to take place of the relative, or protection around the child until the outcome is known. Oh yeah! I'm not advocating we are gods but damn near; if it is not the time for that person to return to spirit then the chances are your prayers to the Egungun and Olodumare will be answered. Your feelings of frenzy, pissed off ness, futility, hopelessness and guilt, or the fact you didn't arrive in time won't turn you into a veggie. These feelings will be greatly diminished because you have been talking to Olodumare through your regular Egungun rituals, prayers, and conversations. Truth!!! "… When I am home I must make sure my Ancestors approve of the way I'm going …" Angelique Kidjo DVD by Shanachie the World Collection

Egungun worship can be a daily ritual along with your morning prayers and/or the morning routine; if you work at night and your routine starts in the evening its o.k. Egungun are flexible (they have not forgotten you or that work happens all hours of the day) say your prayers before you go to bed and avoid nightmares. They remember what swing shift was. Ask for clarification of a situation, or ask to speak to someone in particular, they come in you dreams.

One more way to Honor your Egungun and those of the Community which would be much more public is through an Ancient custom the Libation Ceremony.

The Libation Ceremony is to show Affinity Egungun (Ancestors) reverence (those Ancestors of Good Character and not necessarily of your bloodline). Primarily they should be acknowledged, before any gathering, meeting and/or ceremony, gets underway. It is respectful, healing, humbling, revenant and important to place everyone in the same positive spiritually protective space; to aid in positive communications.

By participating in calling on past Chiefs, Mentors, Musicians, Teachers, Political and/or Historical Ancestors, Loved Ones and Heroes that everyone can share in the calling. Seriously this will elevate the whole proceeding to a higher spiritual plane; or dimension. Sure they will look at you funny but this is what our Egungun want RECOGNITION/RECONCILIATION.

SURE YOU COULD SAY IT'S JUST MY ANCESTORS, BUT I THOUGHT ABOUT THAT UNTIL MY EGUNGUN IN DREAMS KEPT ON SPEWING THIS BOOK TO BE FINISHED FOR ALL THAT ARE SEEKING. I DID WHAT I WAS TOLD!!!

Example: Imagine an African wedding where the grooms' father has past away and/or the brides' mother has past away. The couple has mixed feeling of happiness about their pending marriage and sadness because their parent is missing this important event. However by participating in a ceremony and divination; which includes Libation prior to the wedding they can ask for blessing from their Egungun to guide the marriage, this will go a long way to ease tension. Because both parents are acknowledged; this adds a new depth to the ceremony and the parents will be in attendance in spirit. EGUNGUN RECOMMEND DOING THIS PRIOR TO SETTING THE DATE, YOU BOTH MAY HAVE SOME WORK TO DO. In turn the act of Libation for Egungun can place everyone attending in an elevated mind set. What a unifying and spiritually bonding experience for all that participate.

Did you ever wonder where pouring the first drink on the ground to our fallen/passed, family and friends (homies) comes from? Possibly it's Ancestor Memory, recognition ceremony, in respect for the dead and fallen.

At the end of this work you will discover the reason my Egungun made me write this book. It wasn't just for me even though I am glad they kept on me, but my Children, Family, and Friends of the family will have a gift from beyond this dimension.

++ Also in my seeking I was impressed by the information and what can be drawn out of the wisdoms of those Affinity Ancestors. What you have already read will help you to understand the following chant.

++ THE MANDALA OF THE MYSTIC LAW

"A woman who takes efficacious
Medicine will be surrounded and
Protected by these four great
Bodhisattvas at all times
When she rises to her feet,
So will the Bodhisattvas and
When she walks along the road,
They will also do the same.
She and they will be as in-
Separable as a body and its shadow,
As fish and water, as a voice and
Its echo, or as the Moon and its
Light. Should these four great
Bodhisattvas desert the woman
Who chants Nam-Myoho-Renge-Kyo?
They would incur the wrath

Of Shakyamuni, Taho, and all

The other Buddhas of the ten

Directions"

—Major Writings of Nichiren vol. 3 pg 58

Olodumare will punish the Orisha in the same way! We are not deserted by Olodumare, even though it sure feels like it; we are to respect others as well as ourselves. The above quote is one of my favorites from the time I spent studying Buddhism, because it shows the commitment of the spirits that walk with you on this journey and destiny you chose.

REMEMBER THESE
UNTRUTHS AND RUMORS:
REPARATIONS OVERDUE

African people don't like Black African people in America (crap nobody likes every body). They wanted to keep us in the dark and not travel, while they destroyed our Continent.

African people haven't contributed anything useful to society or the World (double crap). These lies kept us feeling inferior, and under control.

How our men treat our women and children with disregard is based on an African model (crap-where have we been for the last few centuries). To perpetuate the slave model of disrupted family and to put in place the institutions (i.e. child protective services, court system, financial system, educational system) to keep us apart and think it was normal.

Africans are savage and morally degenerate (crap whose example are we surrounded by!). You see enough Tarzan movies and you think we need some white guy swinging from a tree to save us.

How our women treat our men and children with disregard is based on an African model (again crap). When you have strongly defined roles for each member of a society there is no need for family services.

Africans are useless eaters and need to be removed from this society (triple crap). What do you think they have planned to get rid of a people they feel has out lived their usefulness? Use them for medical experimentation, organ donation, incarceration, addict to designer drugs (prescription and street), mis-educate, and feed only scrapes.

How our children treat their elders and their parents is based on a Black African Model (born into a corrupt and disrespectful society leaves little to the imagination). Create a society that treats a people like children and fools, breaks down any respect for authority, pass laws that allow a child to be the parent.

These negative images of us have been ceaselessly feed to the World and us for centuries; which dictate how much trauma we live with on a daily basis.

This in turn affects our relationships and how we view our value in society, also how society views our value. This brainwashing has been performed by experts in deception and the manipulation of media, education, history, and trust, to make damn sure there are very few positive images (we see they are working overtime to wipe out any positive Black images as we know). Damn do they time travel too!

The way we assimilate so well in this primitive culture, is a credit and also a curse, that's called survival or "the Stockholm Affect" (that is when the captive develops sympathy for their captors). How can we continue to give credence to a culture that is bent on our total destruction, genocide, and regentrification at every turn, either by their hand or our own? "The secret of life is to have no fear …" Malcolm X, I believe felt that seeking change and spiritual truth was needed for our people even if it meant his life.

There is an enemy who masquerades in our midst, and, they have our destruction in mind and they are moving at a feverish pace to extirpate (to uproot, to destroy) us before we can wake up, or get it together, etc … The Historical Conspiracy needs to be recognized for how it plays out daily in our lives. The main drama takes place among ourselves, we have been fed self hate for 600+ years told how to stand, what to say, when to eat, work and sleep, generation after generation, and it's a small wonder we apply that hate to one another. STOP IT!!! We helped to legislate (by vote) more prisons, stiffer sentences, and snitching ($1,000 Crime Stopper awards), etc., which was used to put more of us in lock up, we believed the hype and didn't realize it was to criminalize our populations.

Remember the concentration camps of WWII, and the concentration camps of Hurricane Katrina, they (the National Guard) held the evacuees at gun point? If we are at war, they can set up camps for any reason! Remember Posse Comitatus (a body of men that are called by the sheriff to assist in enforcing the law, no the armed soldiers period), it's gone; now we have the Patriot Act, no more citizen rights. Let's not be naïve. We were the teachers and wet nurses that instruct their children without any mention of our contributions to civilization or historical heroes and heroines. Instead we head up the snitch squads of field nurses, community police, and informers, which have the authority to evaluate, spy on and inspect your homes and lives to pass judge your style, businesses for commercial useful function, meetings are you talking about anything that needs to be stopped in its tracks, churches for any political conversations to take away your 501c3 standing and lives to make damning reports, ruin plans, set up to be seized or to take your children or your life. We work in corporate America and apply stereotypes, white racist standards to recruitment, hiring and interviewing of the Black Africans that apply (don't you realize that you got where you are on the ghost of many!!!) for careers and a chance to get their foot in the door. Awake! Or did you think you got there on merit alone! We have to take a stand to break this cycle, due to the spiritual and karmic ramifications that continue to plague us. We aren't weak or lazy so don't go there!!!

By suppressing our historical Cultural and Spiritual differences with our captors we were able to survive the extirpation and build Nations over and over again for others, now it is time to release that spiritual, culture potency and reinvent ourselves, in order to outlive this unyielding slavery. Reality is, this time it's aimed at our annihilation. Dr. James Smalls, professor of N.Y. City College stated … "Suppress behavior to survive a thing, but to not become the thing" ASE (so be it). We are and have become the very thing everyone of us regrets day by day, bit by bit.

Understanding, how spiritually powerful we were, is not a stretch to figure out why we are so faithful, we build churches on every corner in our neighborhoods, so how can we reacquire our powers and values (for ourselves first)? Not just spirituality for spiritual sake or power for power sake and surely not to oppress others. Developing a new paradigm (one that serves us), for our FUTURE will take all of our two cents. We really can heal the World believe it or not! But not if we remain clueless, and comfortable with the way things are.

ANY PLACE BLACK AFRICANS ARE ON THIS EARTH, WE SHOULD BE PRACTICING HUMANITY AND THE CIVILIZATION OF OUR ANCIENT ANCESTORS (GOOD CHARACTER, MORALS, HELPING THOSE IN NEED, HEALING THIS PLANET AND VALUES). I know it sounds preachy but hey! I couldn't rest. We must use our powers wisely; not for revenge; or retribution leave that in the hands of Olodumare (God). Look! There were ethical protocols built into the customs and traditions we followed long ago. They are still in our DNA. And now that is even under attack.

We can not afford not to do the work; or we will remain enslaved for generations to come, and go on the endangered species list with those other cultures, tribes and species.

THE REASON WE SURVIVED IS TO REMEMBER THE TRUTH, TELL THE TRUTH, LIVE THE TRUTH, TEACH THE TRUTH AND BE THE TRUTH. ASE (So be it) AMEN (So be it)
"... If we did something in unison even if it was wrong it would change the World ..." Honorable Dr. John W. Clarke

There seems to be problems in some Black Africans minds regarding Reparations for the Real Holocaust-Hijacking-Uprooting (Extirpate) and continued active enslavement of Our People in this Country and around the World. Some things we should consider requesting and demanding (not just this generation this is for our Future) are:

- Establish The Bureau of Black African Affairs, Directors and Staff can only be Black African Americans (50% minimum). And they know their Black in their actions, mind and spirit.

- Return all stolen Artifacts and Bones from Ancient Cultures to their owners (us) Smithsonian, Grand Canyon etc.

- We choose and fire our own leaders and vote as a block (with discussion) when possible in perpetuity.

- A family home or land any place in the USA and territories to be gifted by the government and tax exempt in perpetuity.

- Dual citizenship (Africa, Caribbean and America). No restrictions on travel to Africa, West Indies, Haiti, Jamaica, Bahamas etc. Government paid grants available for families seeking their roots (Genealogy).

- True History of Africans contributions to civilizations around the World and the impact of our creativity and wisdom, taught in all schools, workshops, trainings, colleges, public or private, police, military, institutions, bureaus, divisions, departments, corporations until such time everybody is up to speed (approx. 150 years) and stop using us for target practice and excuses that we are just like you. Freedom of Information Act applies in all cases.

- Sovereignty and Diplomatic Immunity (Privilege) in perpetuity, if we are to take seriously our own destiny as a people we deserve the same privileges as any sovereign government dignitary.

- No more experimenting on Blacks with vaccines, Nanno bots, drugs, tracking devices or chips, diseases, designer drugs, radiation, biological, electromagnetic pulses, biogenetic weapons, various sterilization techniques and pharmaceuticals.

- Any financial payments paid in Gold, Euros, Chinese yen, Platinum, Silver or what ever the valued tender is by then.

- Stop the extermination of African Nations by playing on the greed of a few (that is how you got us here); Trade between Africans all over the World unrestricted and regulated by our export professionals.

- Get out of Africa after rectifying the damage caused by planed conflicts, weather altering H.A.A.R.P. (Angels don't play this HAARP by Nick Begich)

- Permanent representation in the United Nations with voting power, and, a place on the Security Council.

- Cease and desist playing both sides against each other both sides lose (no fork tongue or broken treats).

- Free Education: Choice of institution and to build and attend our own (PK-PhD). We will have higher education institutions in every state, and we are exempt from other ethnicities attending.

- To develop and participate in our own Spiritual and Cultural Institutions (we shouldn't have to ask for these basic rights all things being equal; Oh! Yeah they are not).

- Reparations for Post/Pre Traumatic Stress Disorders and the wholesale murder of millions of Blacks during middle passage, and the hundreds of Blacks murdered daily at the hands of some scared, racist official.

"We are tired of getting Smallpox in our Blankets!!!" a metaphor for the constant sabotage we encounter minute by minute, did we even get a treaty?

Now who should contribute to the payment and stability of Black Africans in the Diaspora and Continental Africans: All of the Countries, Corporations, Religious (including the Vatican), Financial Institutions, Media, Pharmaceutical Co., and Museums, etc … that participated and/or profited in the Hijacking trade of Black Africans, and continue to manipulate destructive events against our Black people. Those Black Africans that disagree with us; think they have it too good, or their souls are no longer their own. Remember anyone of the above items will elevate us all to a new standing in the World!!! We stand on the shoulders of our Ancestors that demand payment and recognition for their suffering and contributions to this modern World; not to mention our continued suffering at the hands of their children, maybe we will put a chip in you so we all know who to avoid, the first fifty years is going to be rough. It's not just about you!!! "Power to the People"

"BLACK AFRICAN CULTURE SET FOR THE WHOLE

WORLD AN EXAMPLE OF EXTRAORDINARY

VITALITY AND VIGOR, ALL VITALIST

CONCEPTIONS, RELIGIOUS

> AS WELL AS PHILOSOPHIC, I AM
> CONVINCED,

> CAME FROM THE SOURCE, THE
> CIVILIZATION

> OF ANCIENT EGYPT WOULD NOT HAVE
> BEEN

> POSSIBLE WITHOUT THE GREAT EXAMPLE
> OF

> BLACK AFRICAN CULTURE, AND IN ALL
> LIKELIHOOD

> IT WAS NOTHING BUT THE SUBLIMATION
> THEREOF"

> —Honorable Dr. Cheikh Anta Diop 1959

"A PEOPLE THAT LOOSE CONTACT

OF THEIR PAST, CANNOT POSSIBLY

ENSURE THEIR FUTURE"

> —Babatundi Oba of
> Oyotunji Village South Carolina

EXTIRPATED AFRICANS AND THE MIDDLE PASSAGE

African history prior to the Hijacking (extirpate) is extensive, written, painted on walls and oral; we have a wealth of history so far back the memory is in our DNA/RNA!!! (Another reason we are under attack!). In our History this many of us being enslaved for this long is new in human history and that is why we can not rest in peace.

It (Our History), has been touched on in several publications, generally understated, misstated, stolen, altered, burned up, lost, buried, reworked, plagiarized, and out right lied about. Black Africans in America have been trying to put the pieces of Our History back into our Sovereign hands for Centuries. If we are not careful it will be totally whitewashed and we will not be mentioned at all and the raping of Black Africans will continue. This is what's being used to justify profiling, imprisoning, murdering, objectifying, mis-education and ignoring us. If you rewrite a people's history, intellect, and accomplishments, then reduce them to servitude (as the only option) then selling your pack of lies to the World is an easy task. That people become scorned and irrelevant to the scheme of things. Yes, Ancient African people shared much of their Crafts, Culture, Spirituality, Science, Politics, Mysteries and general knowledge with the rest of the World; Equitably and Readily. This was not the mark of a savage, primitive or backward people.

We went from greatness to obsolesce, now African people live on a Continent that has been turned basically into more desert land (due to weather modification), full of disease (from experimentation), genocide (extermination), more slavery, wars and disunity. Brought there by the; you know whose initials (CDC, WHO, EPA, 666, CIA, EU, FBI, DOD,

UN, NATO, etc. etc. etc.), they want us off the only piece of land that if protected could feed the World as it once did.

I know it sounds like we were too good to be true, but the way I see it there had to be a point when we were over come by envy, jealousy, self importance, and greed at the expense of millions of lives and what did it get us but a sharp stick in the brain.

Ancient African people had conflicts that were settled in a more humane way. If there was a war there were very few deaths; and if we took hostages they had a limit on the length of indentured servitude. Early in our History, we more often operated and considered the spiritual realm in our warring. Higher spiritual vibrations or charkas are not a new concept to us.

For example: If an Oba (King), needed help with planting or harvesting, the villagers and tribal members would assist, if a war occurred the captives would become indentured (contract obligation of work for a specified period of time) servants. Most were treated in a fashion that endeared them to the Oba and they may choose to stay and marry, or released to return home when that was possible, and often earned land (remember I said ancient Africa).

During the period in history before Jesus Christ appeared, 2960–1800 B.C.E. Olmec (Nubian-Kemetic), Africans arrived in the Northern, Central Americas, and Mexico which still has communities of Olmec descendants. The mission was basically trading goods, exchange and share cultural beliefs; learning, teaching and marring the indigenous peoples; not to conquer but to coexist (do no harm) to learn and appreciate. Olmec civilization, now are largely Black African descendents; and one of the many African territories outside the Continent of Africa, settled by Black Africans … loose translation extracted from Honorable Dr. Ivan Van Sertima.

The King of Mali, Abu Bakari II, sent several ships across the Atlantic Ocean; the fleets were sent for exploration purposes, well before the insurgence of the African Hijackings. Mandingo explorers made several trade expeditions to the Caribbean, Central and South America, Panama, Cuba,

Dominican Republic, Honduras and Haiti as well, we navigated the Planet settling in many locations around the World. We didn't get lost!

Things were going well for millennia thousands of Peaceful years; then entered the Barbaric off-Landers; from Europe, Rome and Persia just to name a few culprits. They were overwhelmed with jealousy, and envy because of our beauty, spirituality, humanity, knowledge, brilliance, harmony, culture, mythology, civilization, rituals, lifestyles, grace and accomplishments. Their impatience created dangerous liaisons that we are still trying to overcome.

Current published history has managed to reflect that we had no history and were heathens which they lead us to think about ourselves and that Black African people just ran up to these people hollering; "Boss take all I have known and flush it and lets live in hell." NOT TRUE!!! "African resistance to foreign invasion was pervasive ..." Historical and Cultural Atlas The entire Continent was at some stage of war. Typically who do these invader groups send to weaken the resistance of a People, State, Community, Continent or Neighborhood; you guessed it! Disguised military and missionaries with crosses and hidden agendas. They were charged with pillaging, playing to the greed and recruiting the authorities to gain control. Don't forget those, greedy parasitic opportunist diseases that travel with the host. The Roman occupation of North Africa forced into existence Catholicism and Christianity by using the mythology the Ancient African people.

"The list of wars protecting the African homeland is long; the heroes and heroines who fought were African Patriots whom are now Ancestral figures in various panoplies ..." Historical and Cultural Atlas, there is a short list in the chapter titled "Dates and Events to Remember in Black African History."

All this madness added a new dimension to exploitation, greed, envy, war, eugenics, trade and xenophobia. Once the raping and pillaging was underway (African on African; Caucasian on everybody else), there were other events that started to unfold in Native North America; rediscovering and gentrification of another Continent already occupied. During this period there were entire civilizations extinguished and destroyed in Africa as well as the tragedy of the Native North Americans. This is still the case in Africa as we speak, Congo, Darfur!!!

During this horrendous process, there were African Obas (Kings), that where offered valuables and protection from wars; in exchange for capturing other militant Black Africans for the European, Portuguese and Arabian slave trade.

The Obas, Priest and Shaman were eventually used as scapegoats in history, to take the blame for slavery, to give the needed justification and further divide us, and some did deserve that title of informant. Many new cities were established by Africans (i.e. Abeokuta, Morocco, Angola, Tripoli, etc.) Who were fleeing the extirpators (hijackers, slavers)?

Can you even imagine the most unimaginable of situations: waking up to this nightmare too late, you are stripped of any royal identity; herded into a dark, dank cell, naked; held by strangers, enemies, and foreigners and treated worse than you treat your animals? They viewed us as none human, more animal like and soul less (whom are they describing really?); this was to justify to themselves, the powers that be, and European traders in the Americas, the Pope and anyone else they had to convince that the inhumane treatment of Black Africans was warranted, because we were less than human in their minds. What Next?!!!

Those friends and family members (our Ancestors) were killed in these raids and wars. Therefore, there were no opportunities to honor the dead, as is our custom; hundreds of thousands of people's blood drained into the Earth and began the change in soil, this is before the deadly disjointed Middle Passages took place; which partially explains the unrest of the Spirits and Souls of our people.

After being totally disrespected, humiliated, branded, sexually and homosexually abused, starved, dehumanized and maimed over long periods of time; our people were forced onto ships, like animals to be reprogrammed for captivity and servitude. The ships were previously used to transport animals, opium, grains, and spices; now they held our people "Black Gold", hostages.

We were marched in chains by the hundreds of millions, trying to figure out where our families and loved ones were and would we ever be reunited. How did this happen and how does this keep happening? Our captives were drunken degenerates, ex-servants and prisoners of Europe, Rome, Portugal, Spain and Persia; probably the first time they had any control or responsibility what so ever, custody over valuable cargo or the upper hand in their lives.

"I don't care how tired you are of hearing about slavery, because until we acknowledge it and begin to practice and teach our Spirituality, Rituals, Culture, Compassion, Humor, Act, and History to the upcoming generations we are destining to repeat this S___. And no it will not go away quietly, because of the Ancestral unrest and continual damage that it caused; to our Continent and the well-being of Black African people Right Now!!! Repeat; Repeat; Repeat!!!"

These so called civilized people stole, killed, abused and assaulted more than 250 million Black African peoples to reprogram and break spirit, mind, and body for their control; sounds like a damn HOLOCAUST to me. It's very sad that no one mentions this injustice out loud?

These captors and transporters created the atmosphere of lies and stereotypes to justify to the whole World that our treatment was warranted we are still being treated as if we were a lower species, which is still perpetuated today (i.e. … Elected Officials, Corporations, Hospitals, Drug Companies, Military, Police, Any Country America Trades with, Insurance Co., Financial Inst.), even the Churches, did I miss someone? It will eventually bite them in the a__. New Immigrants coming into this Country legally or illegal are schooled in these stereotypes, in case they are still clueless, Blacks are bad not to be trusted, if we hear of your collaboration you will be deported!

Corporations have silent rules in place to purposely oppress Africans first and everyone else of color next, much worse than the glass ceiling concept; our Government practices institutionalized oppression of Blacks in all aspects of our lives no matter how subtle, (Reparations-An act or the process of repairing or making amends; redress; compensation) Webster Dictionary II. Imagine! The African slave trade is still going on; it's alive and encouraged; who are the new scapegoats? The Black children, homeless, addicted people, young Black African Men and Women. Wake Up!!! Please! The first slave ship was called "The Good Ship Jesus".

African people were held on these rickety ships for weeks and months; their captors and ship captains were basically pirates, ex-felons and opportunist, given the choice of accepting contracts to work off their prison terms and become slave traders, or stay in jail for their various crimes, they chose herding us. Quite a few were ship owners that had a monopoly on the open seas, corporate types that made it their business to retrain and deliver us to land owners or the auction blocks, and land owners that used this opportunity to gain more wealth and status and replace the workers that died and ran off, in this new thriving industry there were many fortunes made for everyone involved up and down the line. Imagine. When the crew got bored; they would bring a few prisoners from the cargo hold and taunt and beat them 'til they succumb to what ever sick sick scheme that was planned or hatched for their entertainment. If too many of us died (jeopardized contracts, reduced money), they would simply battle another ship to capture their prisoners and cargo. African prisoners lost their lives while the pirates fought each other; ships sank with all on board, this is partially what happened in the Middle Passage (the largest watery grave since the Great Flood). Why do you think it took so long for us to play in water or swim (cellular memory)? We give that much water respect. Because of the mind boggling, inhumane, suffocating conditions some of us jumped over board with their precious children, and some stopped breathing on purpose to allow someone else to live, thus committing suicide, now relatively new concept; Heavy huh! These acts enabled others to survive; the survivors were given that responsibility. What a heavy agreement and trust to bestow upon another human being. Also, there were a few opportunities to mutiny, take over the ships, escape and/or becoming pirates themselves. They often freed other captured/hijacked Africans from slave ships, towns and ports. We are virtuous! Another obscure survival activity of the Middle Passages. It's a wonder that we made it through these horrendous experiences, still human beings. We may not realize the total history of these outrageous events, nor, just how many of us succumb to the unspeakable brutalities, but remnants of those times live with us, some on the surface some suppressed. But guess what; our Ancestors want us to understand and not squander or forget their anguish and victories, this will also help us today understand the anguish we have bottled up inside. "Forget the Path and get Lost in the Forest" me. Pacts were made amongst the captured Africans Ancestors, those that would survive these atrocities and make it to foreign shores, had the duty to survive at all cost. Because of this obligation and our word we are here today. Our word is bond, or it use to be. Remember!!! These events do not make us immigrants, remember that.

Did you know of a document called "The Asiento" (contract or license), which dose NOT have an expiration date on it. This license is an agreement between the slave trading countries and the Pope of the Roman Catholic Church (a fee based contract). It serves as the legal means to legitimize slave trade businesses anywhere in the world and a guaranteed percentage of profits. This document was developed specifically for the African slave trade (so much money to be made; and land rights to claim) now it is called Trafficking. The first official Asiento was signed 3/26/1713; long after the hijacking proved to be very profitable. The Kings of England and Spain were to receive ¼ each of the profits; the Pope received ½ profits for each transaction. For a time England and its territories was given a monopoly of acquisition over Spain and its territories for 30 years. The Popes had their hands in the African slave trade as early as 1424 and looking for a way to cash in. Shortly after 1740 the Pope at that time gave the "blessing" for the importation of Africans to the Spanish territories in America.

These following dates are approximate timelines, which the Asiento granted these foreigners, the license or contract to capture Africans overtly (without punishment), and, break and train us to serve their every want. First, make us dependant (butler school, laborers, "mammy" nannies, etc.) in their religious, economical and social structure to build a civilization they needed: Portugal 1424–1890; Spain 1455–1865; England 1512–1880; United States 1598–1900; Holland 1625–1835; France 1602–1890; Sweden 1610–1865; Denmark 1617–1828.

At the end of the Civil War 4/9/1865; and during Reconstruction; the 13th Amendment to outlaw overt slavery was ratified (we didn't vote; couldn't). *The 13th Amendment (Ratified 12/06/1865) Section 1 Neither Slavery nor involuntary servitude, except as a punishment for crime whereof the party shall have been duly convicted, shall exist within the United States, nor any place subject to their jurisdiction. Section 2 Congress shall have power to enforce this article by appropriate legislation.* There were approximately one million Black Africans (freed/cut loose), to wander all over the country. We desperately sought family, children, a way home, relatives, friends and asylum. **Not so fast**, HOLD UP! The new names for the laws governing the slave trade were called "Black Codes", devised to control and track the newly freed Africans. Think this crap still exists? Dah!!! **Black Codes:** are said to control whom we could marry; our spiritual expressions, what jobs we could hold, our family structure, creative inventions, what we could own if anything, business ownership, property ownership limitations, rules for testifying in court, how many of us could be at a gathering (public or private, ha! Still enforced at their will) does the word chattel come to mind? We were barely allowed to participate in any of these activities if it wasn't outlined in the Black Code document, you could be recaptured and sent to any plantation or jail. And at the same time insuring white control at all cost was still in affect. Reconstruction (reconstruct rules of slavery)! Oh!

British and Colonial control over the courts and all aspects of society (then and now) meant they could continue to take African children away from their parents. Example: If some white person needed a bed warmer or nanny or field hand they would deem the parents unfit without acceptable means of support, instant orphan, or their parents were killed during the reconstructing of slavery and probably some war. Oh my! Ready made FREE work-force for whites; the newer reconstruction slavery. Africans were required to have jobs (that were approved by whites, any whites) or be fined and/or sent to jail.

During the 1800's more Africans were imported to South Carolina and Georgia (after an end to slavery was declared) approximately 100,000 per year. The population of Africans grew so large that (you know who?), the

Black or Slave Codes were enacted; to prohibit assembly, education, economic freedom, and/or self defense. This did not stop us from plotting the numerous rebellions. Black Codes also were applied to free Blacks in the North. Blacks were not permitted to cross state lines or move from one county to another. Also must have white people (patrons?) who stood surety for their conduct. No place could Blacks vote or testify against a white person, could not buy or sell alcohol, work as clerks, typesetters or printers. The Supreme Court of South Carolina declared in 1831 the education of Blacks was declared unlawful "This race ... in a state of freedom and in the midst of a civilized community, are a dead weight on the progress of improvement".

This is why whites feel no pain when we are justified in our claims against them.

Whites had only to pay fees and assessed fines to bail out the "Freed Africans" to gain possession of their new slave/servant. Sound like the forerunner of many oppressive institutions including Child Protective Services of present, and the "Glass Ceiling" (originally applied exclusively to African Americans, hoping to pacify us). Black Codes; gives the justification to build more jails, giving their unemployables a job in the industry of incarceration; tracking children and their parents, another industry spying; setting codes of behavior that they themselves couldn't pass. There were specific offenses that if convicted of would suspend your right to vote (we did not have anyway), which was one of the definite goals of Black Codes. The offenses that would free you of your "citizenship" were bribery, burglary, theft, arson, obtaining money or goods under false pretenses? Perjury, forgery, looking them directly in the eye, or bigamy would get you incarcerated. Africans were convicted of these crimes rather guilty or not; would immediately remove you from the voters roll, and relieve you of your property ownership. **Sound Familiar!!!** Only the fully recognized humans were considered citizen and had the privilege to vote. Oppression you bet! Charging us falsely or with exaggerated allegations; got us fined and/or locked up (same as now), seems to be the standard treatment for Blacks. If one gets screwed we all do, no matter where you live. "I do like this country but there has to be changes; to a more spiritual, ethical, and equitable place." Africans had only a few choices to keep their families together, to fight to be recognized as citizens with the perks that went with that, and to receive the freedom and right to vote and live as human beings, who just fought a war for, not to mention Human Rights. Whites did anything to weaken, and sabotage the strength of the African collective. Gee! Are you seeing a theme here? Now their using the same strategy to deny higher education, economical opportunities, a job, from Africans currently "free" or incarcerated and any run-ins with the law (no matter how minor) will lead to further exclusions, now we are taking our own lives.

Because sabotage was important for us to prove a point and gain universal freedoms as recognized human beings; we poisoned wells, destroyed crops, maimed work animals, broke tools, we made, and just took off. Then what came next weren't relaxed restrictions for the wrongs committed against us but, another insane scheme the "nigger tools". What? Africans found or caught by the nigger tool patrols (new occupation) Slave Hunters.

Fugitive Slave Laws were next to be enacted to return runaways to Southern Plantation owners and paid a bounty of $250 per person (in useful shape), to the one who allegedly swore a statement of ownership, any white could, (yeah that gal or boy is mine!). See the problem, free Blacks now are at great risk of being kidnapped for the bounty, and without warrants or recourse.

Truth! Who are they really building the new concentration camps for? This makes our smart Black vote even more critical; vote as a block, and have our own convention. This concept is not new, matter of fact we used that power to encourage the Civil Rights law, to be passed in the first place; so it can be done again. We need new laws and fast.

But if you think this is far fetched, or a fantasy maybe we'll wait until they re-enact the "Slave Codes", which were by far, more restrictive than the "Black Codes," Or are they just under the surface waiting to be sprung?

"Slave Codes", were meant to further restrict Freed Black Africans; from socializing with other Africans that were still considered slaves. Now it's the haves and the have nots'. Free Africans needed licenses, to own guns to hunt to feed their families. We couldn't hold meetings or have school.

No Church services were allowed unless a white adult monitor was in the room. To make it difficult to share ideas, start business, share seeds, share political impressions, share cultural observations, share medicinal healing tips and spiritual visions and beliefs.

Here is another so called justification for them to keep their thumb on our necks. There is an unspoken authority to experiment on our population as a whole (anywhere in the World), but think about the incarcerated African prisoners; gene experiments for DNA/RNA mapping and altering, cloning, sterilization, new vaccines, surgical procedures, new medicines, implanted chips, and organ harvesting. Whoa! Don't forget about the Designer Drugs that have been designed for us. "Oh! That's my other book." They (Pharmaceutical Companies, WHO, FDA etc.), use us to determine the safe dosage of medicines, prior to prescriptions being written for whites; work out the kinks first (pun). As Mr. Dick Gregory has stated (not an exact quote), "... Black people are not kidnapping our young Black Boys of Atlanta and extracting the highest grade of interferon and melanin from their tortured bodies, ..." this substance is naturally produced in Africans to protect us from diseases and infections. They (!) have collected enough to synthesize and study for now. Its (interferon-various proteins that can inhibit the development of a virus in a cell) used to minimize rejection of organs during transplant surgery and Hepatitis C-H. They murdered a tribe of young Africans boys to get what they need to save their lives (mainly the powerful and wealthy). Black people in Atlanta don't believe the right man is in jail. Surely, it's no stretch of the imagination to see that experimentation is a constant threat to our communities who really are the bio-terrorist!

Since we have been designated as animals this attitude and the laws still on the books gives them license; no justification is needed in their minds. Have you questioned the medicine prescribed or asked for clarification of your doctor just to have them tell you "find another doctor if you don't do as I say" or take this drug even if the one you are taking works fine. They are killing us daily, practicing medicine.

Have you noticed how many health problems we have developed than our Ancestors? Have you noticed the medicines or drugs have changed our skin color, made our immune systems weaker, people wearing diapers as adults, malpractice/wrongful death, increased infant mortality, and infertility/sterilization is on the rise?

Calling All Black African Babalawos, Priest, And Priestess The Truly Ethically African Centered, the Spiritual Reincarnations Of Our Ancestors, that Are Well Aware Of These Problems that Exist in our Communities still ++YOUR PEOPLE NEED YOU!!! Mo Dupe! (Thank You)

THE FALCONER AND THE PARTRIDGE

A Falconer discovered that he had captured a partridge in his net. The bird cried out piteously when he approached: "Please, Master Falconer, let me go. If you will set me free I promise you that I will decoy other partridges into your net."

"No," replied the falconer. "I might have set you free. But one who is ready to betray his innocent friends to save his own miserable life deserves, if possible, worse than death."

MORAL: Treachery is the basest crime of all.

THE EAGLE AND THE ARROW

One day a bowman saw an eagle soaring lazily in the sky. Quickly he notched an arrow and sent it whizzing after the bird. It found its mark, and the eagle felt itself wounded to death. As it slowly fluttered down to earth it saw that the haft of the arrow which had pierced its breast was fitted with one of its own feathers.

MORAL: How often do we supply our enemies with the means of our own destruction!

Aesop's Fables, 1968 Magnum Pub

THE WILLIAM "WILLIE" LYNCH LETTER OF 1712 AND THE MAKING OF A SLAVE

(Excerpts from the letter are to follow)

PLEASE READ THIS DOCUMENT IN ITS ENTIRETY!!!!!

This speech was delivered by a white slave owner from Australia, William Lynch, on the bank of the James River (doesn't he make toilet paper?) in 1712.

And the Messages set forth in this letter and training session are still practiced by their descendants and an institution which endures as a rotten truth for us to rectify ... Today!

By William Lynch

"Gentlemen, I greet you here on the banks of the James River in the year of our Lord one thousand seven hundred and twelve. First, I shall thank you, the gentlemen of the Colony of Virginia for bringing me here. I am here to help you solve some of your problems with slaves. Your invitation reached me on my modest plantation in the West Indies where I have experimented with some of the newest and still the oldest methods for control of slaves. Ancient Rome would envy us if my program is implemented. As our boat sailed south on the James River, named for our illustrious King, whose version of the Bible we cherish. I saw enough to know that your problem is not unique. While Rome used cords of wood as

crosses for standing human bodies along its' old highways in great num-
bers, you are here using the tree and the rope on occasion.

I caught the whiff of a dead slave hanging from a tree a couple of miles
back. You are not only losing valuable stock by hangings, you are having
uprisings, and slaves were running away, your crops are sometimes left in
the fields too long for maximum profit, you suffer occasional fires, and
your animals are killed. Gentlemen, you know what your problems are; I
do not need to elaborate. I am not here to enumerate your problems; however, I am here to introduce you to methods of solving them.

In my bag here, I have a foolproof method for controlling your Black
slaves. I guarantee every one of you that if installed correctly, it will control
the slaves for at least 300 years. My method is simple. Any member of
your family or your overseer can use it.

I have outlined a number of Differences among the slaves, and I take
these differences and make them bigger. I use Fear, Distrust, and Envy for
control purposes. These methods have worked on my modest plantation
in the West Indies and it will work throughout the South. Take this simple little list of differences, and think about them. On top of my list is;
[Age], but it is there only because it starts with an A; the second is [Color
or Shade], there is Intelligence, Size, Sex, Size of Plantations, Status on
Plantation, Attitude of Owner, whether the slaves live in the Valley, On
the Hill, East, West, North, South, Have Fine Hair, Course Hair, or is
Tall or Short. Now that you have a list of differences, I shall give you an
outline of action-but before that, I shall assure you that Distrust is stronger
than Trust, and Envy is stronger than Adulation, Respect or Admiration
... The Black slave after receiving this indoctrination shall carry on and
will become self refueling and self generating for Hundreds of years,
maybe Thousands.

Don't forget you must pitch the Old Black Males vs. The Young Black
Male, and the Young Black Males against the Old Black Male. You must
use the Dark Skin Slaves vs. the Light Skin Slaves, and the Light Skin
Slaves vs. the Dark Skin Slaves. You must use the Females vs. the Male,
and the Male vs. the Female. You must also have your white servants and

overseers Distrust, all Blacks, but it is necessary that your slaves trust and depend on US. They must Love, Respect and Trust only US.

Gentlemen; these kits are your keys to control. Use them. Have your wives and children use them, never miss an opportunity. If used intensively for one year, the slaves themselves will remain Perpetually Distrustful. Thank you, Gentlemen."

This address can be read at:
thetalkingdrum.com.

Let's Make a Slave: The Origin and Development of a Social Being Called a Negro.

Let us make a slave a slave. What do I need? First of all we need a Black male, a pregnant Black female and her Black baby boy. Second, I will use the same basic principle that we use in the breaking of horses, combined with some more sustaining factors.

When we do it with horses we break them from one form of life to another; that is, we reduce them from their natural state in nature; whereas nature provides them with the natural capacity to take care of their needs and the needs of their offspring. We break that natural string of independence from them and there by create a dependency state so that we may be able to get from them useful production for our business and pleasure.

Cardinal Principles for Making a Negro

For fear that our future Generations may not understand the principles of breaking both horse and slave, we lay down the art. For, if we are to sustain our basic economy we must break and tie both of the beasts together, the Black and the horse. We understand that short range planning in economics results in periodic economic chaos; so that, to avoid turmoil in the economy, it requires us to have breath and depth in long range comprehensive planning, articulating both skills and sharp perception.

We lay down the following principles for long range comprehensive economic planning:

- Both horse and Black are no good to the economy in the wild or natural state.

- Both must be broken and tied together for orderly production.

- For the orderly futures, special and particular attention must be paid to the female and the young offspring.

- Both must be crossbred to produce a variety and division of labor.

- Both must be taught to respond to a particular new language.

- Psychological and physical instruction of containment must be created for both.

We hold the above 6 Cardinal Principles as truths to be self-evident, based on the following discourse concerning the economics of breaking and tying the horse and the Black together-all inclusive of the 6 principles laid down above.

NOTE: Neither principle alone will suffice. For good Economics, All principles must, be employed for the orderly good of the Nation. "... Keep the Body Take the Mind ..."

"You Keep Your Eye and Thoughts on the Female ... Concentrate on Future Generations ..." "... A brief discourse in offspring development will shed light on the key to sound economic principles. Pay little attention to the generation of original breaking but concentrate on future generations. Therefore, if you break the female mother, she will break the offspring in it's early years of development and, when the offspring is old enough to work, she will deliver it up to you for her normal female protective tendencies will have been lost in the original breaking process ..., and she will in turn train the infant to eat out of your hand also ... When it comes to breaking the uncivilized Black, use the same process but vary the degree and step up the pressure so as to do a complete reversal of the mind. Take the meanest and most restless Black, strip him of his clothes in front of the remaining male Africans, the females, and the African infants, tar and feather him, tie each leg to a different horse in opposite directions, set him a fire and beat both horses to pull him apart in front of the remaining Africans. The next step is to take a bullwhip and beat the remaining African males to the point of death in front of the females and the infants. Don't kill him, but put the fear of God in him, for he can be useful for future breeding ... breed two African males and two African females, then take the two males from them and keep them moving and working. One female bear a female, the other bear a male, both without the influence of male image, frozen with an independent psychology, will raise their off-spring into reverse positions. The one with the female offspring will teach her to be like herself, independent and negotiable ... The one with the African male offspring, she being frozen with a subconscious fear for his life, she will raise him to be mentally dependent and weak, but physically strong-in other words, body over mind." "... We must COMPLETELY ANNIHILATE the Mother Tongue ..." "For example, if you told a slave that he must perform in getting out "our crops" and he knows the language well, he would know that "our crops" didn't mean "our crops" and the slavery system would break down, for he would relate on the basis of what "our crops" really meant. So you have to be careful in setting up the new language for the slaves would soon be in your house, talking to you as "man to man" and that is death to our economic system. In addition, the definitions of words or terms are only a minute part of the process. Values are created and transported by communication through the body of the language ... these many value systems would sharply clash and cause internal strife or civil war, the degree of conflict being determined by the magnitude of the issues or relative opposing strength in whatever form."

There is so much more to this document; i.e. the Breaking Process of the African Women, The Negro Marriage Unit, Controlled Language, and I want you to get a copy and read it in its entirety, makes you sick. But did you read this excerpt from this outrageous document, these steps were immediately put into practice; and is still being enforced and updated as they need it, to re establish mistrust among Black African descendants of slaves, to this very day in 3/8/00. It's a small wonder that we of African Heritage and descent are discounted on every level, and have to fight tooth and nail to stay ahead of this modern day genocide plan; and why our children are being preyed upon, and labeled as dangerous. No matter what status we achieve we are deemed valueless. We must stop perpetuating this doctrine if we are to be taken seriously and be able to really make a difference; by consciously making the effort to redirect these tendencies we've been taught. People new to this Country think the same about us as they do; no real history is being taught, except of course the history that makes us look more vulnerable, valueless and easy to ridicule, so much so we don't even like us.

Government Departments, the European Union (EU) and select Corporations; now more than ever have become the masters of this plantation called United States of America, the World and Planet Earth; with its institutionalized economic authorities are kidnapping our children and our minds; for what purpose now? We must still be perceived as a danger to the scheme. And what are they really doing, what's in the vaccines? What the Hell!!! With reduced employment and business opportunities; drugs were introduced as another means of manipulation and mind control as a source of income for those of us deemed dangerous "jobs and business opportunities" with the goals of blocking Ancestral memories, and further blighting the family structure. Manipulating the stock market, interest rates, credit reports, changing the color of money, the federal reserve, industry developments, and how much money is in circulation on the streets (oh yeah there is a tracking device in the money), this predictably would produce panic in this society at large but too many are in denial. Well, with this much control; it is a small wonder that the most unpopular segments of the country are landowners, educated, wealthy, and upwardly mobile, and have the nerve to think we could run for president. "… If I was president on Sunday … I would be assassinated on Monday …" Bob Marley. What do they do? Set new priorities!!! Create new, more dangerous stereotypes, market crash, change the color of the money again, start another war, massive layoffs and change the value of an education or the lack there of (decide who can or cannot get and education). Soon to be put in place, anyone with a drug arrest or any misdemeanor, felony or any suspected criminal activity will not receive a Pell Grant or any other Grants for College, a job, SBA loan, or any other loans (house, debt consolidation, etc.), don't worry they need us to buy their cars, isn't that interesting you can buy a car but not a house. Also they encourage outsiders to takeover successful African Businesses and Organizations (i.e. … U.L., N.A.A.C.P., B.E.T., and U.N.C.F. etc.). By removing any mark or cultural characterization of the Black owner, it becomes very difficult to leave a legacy or inheritance.

By controlling growth and development of the unborn through the use of bio-engineered hormones, antibiotics and drugs in the food, air, and water this is making us infertile as they are (to this extinct, unheard of in our historical memory) which is also chemically changing our men and women into "body over mind" meat puppets. Lets not forget the old plagues (smallpox, bubonic, typhus, typhoid fever) and the new ones (HIV, AIDS, cancer, infertility, incontinence, suicide) that infect our society today; we can't forget the designer diseases nor the designer drugs that were manufactured to go with them. Oh! Did I mention the United States and the EU are backing slave trade in the Sudan; it's over the minerals, oil and the land. Because this is an attempt to make damn sure they neutralize those of us awake and waking from the devastation of the Willie Lynch indoctrinations.

FIELD AND HOUSE
AFRICAN SLAVES

These terms were designations of placement, these terms were not derogatory terms they were distinctions and necessity during the early decades of slavery. After the hijackers heard there pep speech by Lynch; these terms were the perfect opportunity to further control and divide our Ancestors and us today through hatred, fear, dependency, color, hair and mistrust. These were roles we had to play, not life styles to inflict pain on each other. As the law was set down by, who? Willie Lynch.

Field Africans, where dehumanized, trained, and branded with hot irons like animals, also beaten humiliated and beaten some more. Starved for days, months and years to ensure the break down of resistance, and still forced to labor. Understand this treatment had nothing to do with our ability to learn (as the Bell curve would lead us to believe), or grasp a concept. Our civilized, majestic and stately presence is what civilized the World, thus the ferocious treatment.

Field Africans had to be more physically and mentally strong than their overseers to endure the torturous conditions; such as: mind control, torture, rape, and exposure to the harsh weather (sun, storms, hurricanes etc ...), working from dawn to dawn, no clothes or tools except what they could fashion out of waste materials. Field, did most of the physical labor and inventing equipment and tools (cotton gin, seed planters, harvesters, and, pickers), maintaining roads and buildings, cultivate crops, hunt, animal husbandry, these were skills that were brought with them from home and to utilize information smuggled to them from House Africans.

They stole the complete spectrum of our societies and cultures; Calvary, Doctors, Priest, Babalawo, Priestess, Negotiators, Herdsman, Herbalist, and Field were Co-Organizers of many uprisings and revolts. In America, we were not allowed to marry, keep our children (like it is now), and raise a family or to be taught to read and write (it meant death if caught). Due to white fear of an African taking over; and everything being equal there should have been a few openly Black African Presidents by now. Ha!

When and if anyone rebelled (which we did as often as possible) they would choose the fiercest person or child to brutally and publicly execute to keep everyone in line per Lynch. Fields' had a harder time during the end of the Civil War. Partially due to limited access to minimal education, or to receive an approved work situation sanctioned by those in charge, thus stigma (Black-Slave Codes). The newly Freed Africans had a tremendous thirst for knowledge, hoping that education would assist them to achieve some respect and the means to raise and take care of family oh yeah that's when that forty acres and a mule came in, NOT. Many became teachers for this very reason; "Each One Teach One".

House Africans were also dehumanized, branded like animals, trained as spies, brutalized daily, humiliated, later forced to teach Catholicism. They also were beaten and beaten, starved while preparing meals for their overseers (not even allowed to eat scraps, for months and years shaped into servants and to be able to perform as forced labor when ever the need arose. Understand it had nothing to do with the ability to learn or grasp a concept; Black Africans civilized the World; so this torturous treatment had everything to do with our utter magnificence and the fear of the overseers. Yes!

House Africans, had to be able to portray humbleness (seen and not heard), humility, agreeableness, confidentiality 24/7, (kept secrets on both sides), without letting what they've heard or witnessed effect their outward demeanor. House Africans cooked, made clothing, cleaned, served, were raped, used as bed and foot warmers, wet nurses; and, stole food to give to the Fields, they were go betweens, stole books-learned to read and taught (on the sly at the risk of death) the Fields, also Co-Organizers of many insurrections. House, were also involved in the gathering of information such as times of events, and, upcoming sale of Africans from the captors; responsible to assist in the planning and strategy to escape with the Fields.

Yes! Also, they had to provide cover or a cover story for escaping Africans; and often died at the hands of the plantation owners due to the oath of secrecy, between Africans.

There was also brutality, public executions and lynching of House and Field as well. No one escaped this insanity rather House or Field or any place we were in the world. Another interesting fact about the Field and House designations was that the women bore the children of the master and often saw them sold right from under them as punishment and to keep us in line, also the lighter skinned children occasionally had property left to them and were able to be educated later in the 1800's. House, were able to find, better jobs after the Civil War only because they had managed to become Legally Literate and identifiable to the employers. Both groups of our Ancestors were constantly rapped by white men and women, old and young, it was also common to be accused of some offense i.e. he/she looked me in the eye, he/she talked back to me, he/she touched me, and not have a clue about the accusations. The same things are happening to us today! Remember those men and women saying "it was a Black man that killed my children, or killed my wife/husband" nothing but lies, they were the guilty ones. And some Black person ends up in jail or killed by some angry mob, there are many names that would fill a book because of false accusations by whites; remember Emmett Till, who supposedly whistles at some white women and ended up beaten to death. I have a profound respect for these two groups of our Egungun, because today where ever we find ourselves in this society there is no trust or respect for each other, to even pull off a coup d'etat, or plan a coup de grace.

Both the Field and House Africans were charged with the colossal task of remembering our history. We were accomplished in the art of Oral Tradition (the truth by mouth to ear communication) passing our history (names of Kings, customs, legends of heroes, and traditional beliefs), forward to next generations.

The name of this specialized group of Africans is called Griots by all of the various Black African audiences. They were responsible for remembering our history in this new land and seeing to it being passed down. You see the information, history, culture, traditions and secrets worked well in this oral tradition, only we knew what we were saying; we still use this practice today (Ebonics, Rap, Jive, Jone'n etc.). This is why we had so much distrust for written contracts, a hand shake and your word was bond.

Another very important task that was to be performed by the Obas (Kings), Babalawos, Priest, Priestess, Griots and Elders (Field and House representatives); of various tongues and tribes was to, come together to make sense of this situation in secret so we can understand how not to repeat this calamity. There became an urgent need to plan and agree on just how we would respond to certain problems we faced daily so we could present a united face. How we would conceal and homogenize our cultures, traditions, spirituality, language, and customs in order to preserve what they could, thus the camouflage or cloaking of important traditions under the English language and under the Christianity guise. Others (Field and House), were designated to keep track of who was sold to whom; who was born and who were their parents or where they were transported and sold; this also fell under the custom of the Griot. Have you married a relative? How the Hell would you know!!! Do you love each other and just can not stop fighting and arguing, I know too simple. There are several ways the Ancestors have tried to notify us: 1. by being sterile, until you changed partners. 2. by not being able to get a long with each other no matter what. 3. By producing bad dreams. 4. By creating accidents when really stubborn etc. If you have any questions regarding your relationship go for divination; you will find out.

During those times the Ase (power) of Olodumare (God truth) was called upon to unify all Africans in Faith, Spirituality, Culture, Values, Commonality and Morality; which played the role of inclusion of all of us not to exclude any Black Africans from putting in their two cents; this fact was held close by both Field and House, Why? Same boat, same experiences, and same deceptions remember. Christianity was developed out of the total cultures of the African people (thousands of years B.C.), then artfully used our own culture, traditions and spirituality and mythology to oppress us and the whole World. Then we in turn artfully used their Christianity to conceal and cover our Power and Truth to preserve our beliefs and culture. Now after hundreds of years of mistrust we have grown accustom to the various religions of Christianity and have lost our Destinies, Power and Truth. Has anything changed for us? Are we still looking for freedom? Are our lives as a whole more secure? No! We are living in a masterful hologram. We must remember that our healing will bring about the healing of this planet from Earth to Heaven. Therefore, you/we owe it to ourselves, your family and the Ancestors; to investigate to figure out what's' missing; believe me, they are, working hard to figure out; what can they do to keep this powerfully creative people pacified?! The powers that be work over time to think of ways to totally defeat us; therefore we can not afford to hibernate. Certainly you don't want the slave masters to be more familiar with our spirituality than ourselves, nor should we allow them to continue to oppress us with it. Please! Pick up a book and read a little, you will be surprised at the people that think they know us well enough to write about US; even you with your skepticism; you will be impressed and guess what you can write a book too. Haven't the Ancestors talked to you with some life saving messages before?!

We still are suffering from such issues of anger that most of the relationships we have control over we display this anger in the most unnatural ways. On a cellular (DNA/RNA) level we experience fresh pain, which is real. Due to what we call Post Slavery Trauma Syndrome (whites can not cure it). Don't go to the white Psychiatrist expecting them to have a clue; they have no frame of reference, and have no idea what the Hell you're talking about, they will give some dangerous designer drugs. Seventy five%-Eighty five% of our People were raped at will (anytime, day or night); Thirty%-Forty% of our People were homosexually attacked at will (anytime, day or night). 100% of our People were in the same boat. What choices are we making, Ancestors are humiliated for us. This insanity really had to be denied and suppressed in order for us to carry on and survive; WE JUST CAN NOT FORGET!!! It's written in our Ancestral memory so the gap will continue to grow between us until a major Spiritual cleansing and healing occurs. They did this to the Field and House Africans; so you see none of us got off easy. STOP THE BLAME GAME!!! We must forgive each other, and not forget other wise this insanity will repeat, until the Truth is told and we can take our rightful place; the heads of this nightmare must pay. Because when we are healed we can bring peace to the lands. We are our Egungun (Ancestor), and our children display their discontent with this world and our plight.

LIGHT A HOLY FIRE

Receive this Holy Fire,
Make your Lives like this Fire,
A Holy Life that is seen,
A Life that has No End,
A Life that darkness does not overcome,
May this Light of God in you Grow
Light a Fire that is Worthy of your Heads,
Light a Fire that is Worthy of your Children,
Light a Fire that is Worthy of your Fathers,
Light a Fire that is Worthy of your Mothers,
Light a Fire that is Worthy of your God.
Now go in Peace.
May the Almighty Protect you today and All Days

—Masai, Tanzania

FOR THE LIVING DEAD

O GOOD AND INNOCENT DEAD, HEAR US:

HEAR US, YOU GUIDING, ALL KNOWING

ANCESTORS, YOU ARE NEITHER BLIND NOR

DEAF TO THIS LIFE WE LIVE: YOU DID

YOURSELVES; ONCE SHARE IT. HELP US

THEREFORE FOR THE SAKE OF OUR DEVOTION,

AND, FOR OUR GOOD

—MENDE, SIERRA LEONE

EXPLODING THE MYTHS AND LITTLE KNOWN FACTS ABOUT RELIGION

"YOU ARE THE SUM TOTAL OF ALL OF
YOU'RE BELIEFS AND YOUR BELIEFS ARE ALWAYS
SUBJECT TO CHANGE AS YOUR KNOWLEDGE BASE
EXPANDS MOST PEOPLE REFUSE TO ACCEPT A
NEW BELIEF SIMPLY BECAUSE IT CONTRADICTS
THEIR PRESENT BELIEF SYSTEM TO CONTINUE
TO BELIEVE IN A PROVEN FALSEHOOD IS
   DETRIMENTAL
TO THE BELIEVER ONE MUST NEVER BE AFRAID
TO EVALUATE NEW INFORMATION AND ACCEPT
IT IF IT IS PROVEN TO BE TRUE."

—From the Browder File by Anthony T. Browder Pg 51–53

ANCESTRAL MEMORY AND PAST LIVES

This phenomena of Ancestral Memory and Past Lives, is, that which we have experienced and inherited from our past lives. Heredity on a cellular level, DNA stores our past lives, cultural traits, traditions and Ancestral memories. We were born again!!!! Truly

This is why Ancestor reverence is so vital. We want good circumstances during this lifetime, but we keep making the same mistakes in our lives and/or families; generation after generation. Why?

Because, we are our Ancestors, and we have not put into practice what we have learned, with the absence of Ancestral worship we are ignoring how proud we should be of our accomplishments, creativity, and sense of justice on a massive scale. Your Egungun will write a book for you and your descendents if you are willing to listen they are screaming for us not to fall into the same old pits. Overt slavery was abolished, we tried to reunite the family, we protested injustice i.e. voting rights (we vote they do not count our votes), passed civil rights act (which has been diluted to include those that have no understanding what this country owes us) that expires every ten years, what is that?!

There is so much money being made by Psychologist; from Black people that are looking for understanding and answers to what is happening; or who they are, or what are these voices in my head telling me, or what does this dream mean and why am I here?

Psychiatrist and Hypnotist are getting wealthy on Misdiagnosing and over medicating us, at our expense. We can remember our previous lives as Men or Women; Kings and Queens, Chiefs or Priest, Eunuch or Concubine, Field or House, Free or Slave. Oh yes if you want you can!!! It kind of stands to reason why, our children seem to be lost and out of control and vulnerable because, We Are. ASE There is a strong connection to our mental health and our spirituality, because we are on a spiritual vibration that emanates from our melanin.

We continue to spiral in a downward direction due to our own mistrust of each other and our lack of homage we talk to each other but do not listen. Egungun; are quiet tired of us crapping and stepping in it. They want to help, just call. They did not go through hell for us to become extinct; if we continue to (ignore how we practice the W. Lynch) hate ourselves, we are not acknowledging our true potential. I share this information with you because I kept asking the question, Why the Hell don't we work to respect each other? Why do we think it's funny to see our brothers and sisters in trouble and pain? W. Lynch is only responsible for introducing this evil plan but we are the ones that perpetuate it every day. So if we can remember when we were great then maybe we can unite and get some agreements made between ourselves. Let us be the ones that initiate these Continental saving measures. We have learned how to cover up guilt with enough laws, legislation, and money; trust me we will never have enough ducets to sweep this inequity under the rug, even though people are trying to make us forget, and feel guilt or childish for even bring it up. This trend is definitely reversible but there is a price and work involved. I know that some of us like being comfortable and are not thinking about those that are not. We can not become the captors or we will become wiped out. A Big No, No. Do not marginalize your selves, for a reward, and don't think just because you pass away you won't be back, to repeat this hell again. What do they call it oh yeah the Stockholm syndrome.

Depending on the severity of our family histories and current conditions; a reputable Babalawos' divination is first on the agenda; reason; so they can let you know where to begin and what needs to be rectified in your family to save lives. Understand it may take generations. So Start! Oh Yeah you don't have to cash in your wealth or position, just get a better understanding of what needs to be the priority and put it in place. Every one of us has a role, and it is not to make our enemies rich off our sweat any more!

This is why massive reparations from ROUND THE WORLD are owed to US (you and me); By Those EXTIRPATORS: Corporations; Catholic Church (Vatican); Bankers; Insurance Companies, etc.; that pretended their innocent of any complicity in the crimes against Black Africans. "Oh no we don't owe you people anything!" Or "I wasn't even born yet!" They are wrong; and so are you if you believe the same thing!!! Remember what W. Lynch said "… teach your children to do the same"; they did and continue to this very day even when it seems like their hypnosis isn't working they step it up.

Ancestral memory and our past lives; include but not limited to DNA/RNA, cellular memory which also houses our intuition, refinement, civilization, values, culture, traditions, mental training, development, education and Spirituality; which is embedded in our entire population; that is not unique to us only; but we just have a different calling for this date in time it is to Heal A Nation of Black African People.

The Griots' of today that I have listened to and shared are (just to name a few): the Last Poets; Gil Scott-Herron; Nikki Giovanni; Royal Empire; Royal T; Sista Soulja; Professor Griff; Jadakas; Mary J. Blige, Mos Def, and a variety of other Rap Artist (not the slang of Hip Hop), poets and actors. We have to support and encourage the Oral Tradition of our Ancestors and not let this suppression of our Truth Sayers (Griots) continue. And I am not speaking on those that sell their art and truth for a scandalized contract, that the label dictates lyrics, men in dresses, facade and lifestyle insuring a short professional life.

Our relationships with authority (police, agencies etc.), our love relationships; how we learn (visually and by vibration); and what we value, our responsibilities to family, and many more are issues that cry out to be addressed by us all. We all have what is called the 'reverse mind' effect, from the Willie Lynch doctrine. When we find ourselves automatically saying or doing something that, we feel deep down deserves an apology and that person really didn't earn our wrath, it isn't us; we should be asking "where did that come from?" or "why did I say that?" or "why have I left my family unguarded?" You have already endured the shame so do something to remedy the situation, and protect those children.

Why is it that some people we encounter seem to draw from us extreme sympathy or the unexpected worse behavior that we ever displayed. It, maybe due; to the relationships we've had from a past life scenario. Maybe that boss still thinks he/she is your master! They have baggage to atone for as do we; and NO we can not do it for them or excuse their behavior.

Take heed Our Ancestors are trying to get our attention and tell us something, before the real sadness comes.

During our lives as we get older, we are starting to realize that circumstances seem and are quite dire, arguments and problems all sound familiar, we are still fighting wars, with other black and brown peoples; as it was when we were children. "What goes around comes around". Except we forgot why our Grandparents, Parents, Children, and Ancestors, taught us the dangers of certain activities, or being mindful of the company we keep, where we should be or not to be; don't forget to pass it on, this is critical for our children's safety and that of generations. At the end of our lives we may pray, saying to God, "Please Elevate My Life and Our Families Lives and Destinies to a much Higher Plane because this 3rd dimension stinks; we must not forget; we are Your Favorite!" Yet when we incarnate again things may seem ridiculously worse, that's because we are gathering as much as we can (hoarding), because we have gone without for so long.

But tell me; who else is going to Stop this Merry Go Round if it isn't we. It's easier buying a car than a house! Why?

Ancestral memory and past lives play a heavy role in how we have adjusted to the lives we lead. Delusions of grandeur can be real, just in the wrong time.

In Africa there is still evidence of a long standing practice of placing an identifying mark on the body of the dead; so that the living will recognizes the person when they return as the new born? You would be surprised how many return with the identifying mark on their body. Heavy Huh!

Birth being the first in a series of Rites of Passages; this is why midwives that are culturally in tune with the parents and tradition is most important when coming in contact with this child for the first time (Oh yeah you can dictate how your child will enter, soft drums or jazz, fragrances, soft lighting-you get the point). No, white girl or guy; spending vacation or peace corps in Africa doesn't count; they tend to think they are Blacker then you are.

When you are dealing with an old Soul you want to give the child as much sensitivity and care as possible. And for those frightened women that are not interested in having the child, there should be a private atmosphere where they can think about the future of the child; "I will keep the baby" or "I will adopt my baby to another black family" or "my extended family will raise my child". Options! Please we can not keep letting foreigners raise our children; there is more at stake than just cultural considerations.

Some of the Black children that are placed with a non Black family disappear around 9 years old (from Egungun).

There is a reason we have asked the Gatekeeper (Oni Bode), to be here at this particular time in history. It has been nearly 700 years since this wholesale Slavery insanity started on a Worldwide plan of One People, US; being annihilated we realize, and have shown we need help, from a greater source than ourselves, to change this maddening situation; and alleviating this karmic debt we are under. We can not keep passing it on or we will be extinct. Some dismiss this tragedy by saying "get over it", well I dare you be so simple, while some of us are trying to figure out away to heal most if not all of us. Really! As you can see I don't have the answers I just raised more questions; so lets' keep talking.

I have written this book at the behest of my Ancestors; to help heal my family and the families of other Africans; to relieve our collective karmic debts. All of those questions I had as a child are getting answered. What I am proposing here is to incorporate some things of our past that are strongly requested by our Ancestors; (a). Directed prayer; (b). Total healing; (c). Ancestor reverence and Atonement by us, (d). Incorporating rites of passages, (e). Remembering the rituals that made us strong not infamous, (f). Our presence in this day in time is for a profound reason, (g). Be active not stagnant, (h). Don't think you can not be a change agent, (I). Think before we speak, the influences are strong (the Lynch swindle), (j). We must save as many of our unborn as possible, (k). When we are wronged speak out and do not give in, Boycott that day, i.e. the company, or do not shop, or stay home; all of us. Oh Yes! I do believe this is possible.

Some of us will not see the value (your too comfortable, or your in so much pain, or you believe the lies that we have been told that Blacks are no good), but what we're talking about will ultimately change mankind for the better; but US first. The sleeper must awaken, (with a plan). Back to Dune the Movie

There are those Africans that will be elevated and changed for the better, in spite of their arrogance. The truth is we Africans in the United States have been imbued with knowledge for all peoples; and we have only mis-used it; we are the caretakers of the Planet, like it or not; all Africans need to participate in some kind of mass spiritual awakening which will heal all peoples. You already know where the opposition will come from.

Firstly, We Black Africans, have to stop the fight over what to call ourselves, because we are Africans who were removed from our African Continent a long time ago; however we are currently calling America home because we live here, no disgrace; it is o.k. we are here. We must not forget our African Ancestors are not at all totally satisfied. "Honor thy Father and Mothers that their days be long ..." Regardless what ever plane their on, remember you do not have to forget just sincerely forgive.

Next, we must stop thinking the rules of this society considers us as having a viable role. On every conceivable level we are excluded (why do our civil rights have an expiration date, and can you imagine that what they do in their bedrooms has now won a place in a law against slavery!!!!). Don't get upset that is just the way it is for now. We must recognize that this society (we have assimilated) prefers to dispose of whatever or whomever they have used up or deemed useless eaters. The presentation by Willie Lynch "Making of a Slave", is still alive and well; each generation is introduced and taught about its devastating effect, directly or indirectly. We have allowed so much moral decay to occur, that our Ancestors barely recognize us, and we struggle to "Know thy Self". We have been forced to live in the lower emotional realms for so long that we have forgotten how elevated all our existence were. Oh yes! You can manipulate the words and dismiss this work as you like; but understand that our Ancestors and God will not let them assimilate on a spiritual level until they atone to us. And we are not off the hook; respect ourselves there is no getting around it, because it is long overdue. Ancestors deserve it and so do we; don't you agree? Matter of fact my Ancestors and Olodumare wouldn't let me rest until I finished with this 1st book. There are books in a lot of us.

Think of it, would we be able to survive any of the horrors that our Ancestors endured? I think not. We would be extinct by now if we were not made of stern stuff. We have been isolated so long we are a new tribe! Funny thing about a tribe there is the element of survival of the group, and discipline with in the group, without interference from the outsiders.

However, the Past Lives we've lived and the Ancient African Ancestral Memories are alive and well; we have just ignored and suppressed them; which have proven not to be very smart. When your child comes up to you and says they have a messages for you Listen; when that voice says call so and so they are in trouble and need your help Listen. Africans around the World have a collective memory and a collective future; how can we continue giving aid to the Africans and they are worse off then ever. Not knowing who we are leaves all of us exposed and vulnerable and on the verge of extinction. All of the starvation, genetic genocide, mass murders, and ethnic cleansing of Africans seems as though we are being used as human sacrifices for some one else's survival surely not for ours. Oh another mystery; are we living through some spiritual gauntlet, to establish that unique and powerful connection we have enjoyed with Olodumare (God); lets pay this karmic debt before we are no more. None of us has any more negative baggage than the other, we must do something about it; time is so short and no one somebody has the answers.

PREPARATION FOR PUBLIC AND PRIVATE EGUNGUN (ANCESTOR) WORSHIP

There are basically two types of Egungun rituals: Libation; which are usually performed at public events, and, Ritual; which is more for Ancestor Societies, Personal and Family Worshipping.

The Libation ceremony (Public) can be as short or as formal as you have the time to dedicate. Start by compiling a list of as many Affinity (Persons like family not in bloodline) Ancestors as possible; they can be specific to the event at hand or anyone that is admired by the group. Example: An Author and/or Poets conference, you may call upon; Langston Hughes, Cheikh Anta Diop, James Baldwin, Zora N. Hurston, Rev. Samuel Johnson and others to give reverence. At a Kwanzaa celebration calling possibly on, Shirley Chisom, Ossie Davis, Johnny Cochran, Marcus Garvey, Matthew Henson and so on.

FORMAL PUBLIC LIBATION CEREMONY:

- Explain briefly your purpose for the gathering.

- Designate an Elder or Spiritualist to call the names of the selected Ancestors.

- Greeting Good Morning/Evening Date Year

- Purpose of Libation briefly explained. "To honor and respect to those that came before …"

- A way to get the participants involved is to choose someone to sprinkle cool water (omi tutu) on a plant or on the ground for each name called. The gathering can say ASE (so be it) or Amen (so be it), in unison after each name called.

- To bring more harmony to this event allow those willing to call upon Ancestors from their own families or their heroes.

- Lastly, say "we call upon you with honor and respect, and we ask for your blessings for a successful gathering". You will experience a very good meeting as a result of taking a few minutes to acknowledge Egungun; we all are gathered here in harmony. If someone gets up and leaves they should not have come.

TRADITIONAL EGUNGUN CEREMONY:

This ceremony can be as involved or as basic as you like. This is a good opportunity to ask those Elders in the family before they become Egungun, to provide you with as many names as they can remember. You need to compile a list of as many Egungun (Ancestors) as possible. You can use nicknames or even Great Grand ...; if their exact name is not known at this time; someone will have the answer for you, Ancestors!

PERSONAL EGUNGUN CEREMONY:

- There should be a separate list made for your Father's side of the family and another for your Mother's side, because you call them separately.

- With your two list in hand we can start;

- Good Morning/Evening Egungun Date Year Occasion or New Day

- I, (_____) am your descendant.

- I/We are here to honor you.

- Egungun on my Father's side: Sprinkle cool water (OmiTutu), on a plant or the ground; before and during the calling out loud of each name.

- If other family members are present they should say their names and duties can be shared; (sprinkling of water and tapping with sticks [Opa Egun] or cane on the floor). This summons Ancestor spirits. Tyler Perry's Family Reunion DVD has a scene in the bonus material of his movie to illustrate this point.

- After each name is called say "I/We give respect." Do this for each name called rather you knew them or not. Fathers side first then Mothers side.

- Next give prayer to both sides for those that perished in the Holocust, Wars, Revolts, Middle Passage, Malpractice, Racism; those whose names have been forgotten; those who were Miscarried, Premature Death, Aborted, Stillborn or Born Abiku (infants that die shortly after birth).

- Lastly give prayer and/or concerns and problems of the family. Add any thing you would like, especially how the family is doing. This can be done out loud.

- Then close by saying; "I praise all those in Heaven". Thank You!

You can use this time to humbly apologize for any abortions that may have occurred due to our lack of knowledge or arrogance. Black African people deeply believe in reincarnation; therefore that action may have been stopped with a better understanding and that Egungun (Ancestor) will have to arrive at a later date. This will start to heal any guilt we may have; men and women. Also you may take these opportunities to start healing the whole family; of undesirable habits, estrangements, enemies, curses and addictions, rather than confronting that particular individual. **No, this isn't magic; the person must want to live, and stop trying to commit a slow suicide. That's on them!**

Sincerely praying to Olodumare (God) and your Egungun (Ancestors) will begin to heal relationships and issues in the family as well as between the living and the dead. Health problems that seem to plague, generation after generation; can be resolved with serious prayer, divination and their remedies. This is a very empowering feeling, and it takes work, but guess what; it's worth it.

The saying "… from your mouth to God's ears …" They are around you anyway might as well utilize them.

The sacred number for Egungun is nine (9), it just is! You will notice that the items and offerings to Egungun usually is nine. There are several of the recommended readings that have drawings of altars that may help to inspire you.

When you discover that your Ancestor Altar needs a permanent location in your home, here might be one way to figure this out. Sit quietly in your home and concentrate on whether or not you want to be the anchor in the family, because it is a lot of responsibility. While meditating; consider a place that will not be disturbed by anyone except you, and occasionally the family.

Egungun prefer constant white light (candle, night light etc).

If you are married you should encourage your spouse to construct an Egungun altar for their family as well.

Clean and smudge with smoke using sage thoroughly. Clean floors and walls with cool water (omi tutu) add 9 drops of ammonia and a little cinnamon to the water. This process or ritual draws you closer and focuses your intent because the goal is to eliminate negative energies.

Then to contain the power of your altar, use African chalk (Efun) or regular chalk to draw a circle around the altar space from wall to floor. In completing this cleansing ritual will consecrate and contain the Ancestor spirits that will be drawn to your altar; this is a special place that you can go to commune with your Ancestors and they will be there for you.

Now you are ready to start layering the elements for their altar. Your Ancestor altar can start off very simply, Oh Yes! It will expand and grow in size. Some elements you may include are suggestions: The Urn with the cremated remains should be placed on your altar as well; White cloth/sheet, placed on the floor; vase of white flowers 1 or 9 or any that grow in your garden; any pictures of the Ancestors (only use those pictures that have no living person with the Egungun in them); the light source; toys for infants that had been lost due to Miscarriages, Stillbirths (Abiku), or Abortions; bowl of cool water (omi tutu) or 9 glasses of water; bowl of 9 pieces of fruit; any thing they may have enjoyed in life; coffee with cream and lots of sugar; glass of whiskey and/or their favorite alcoholic beverage; any of their belongings (hats, canes, shoes, ties, cologne, after shave, clothing, jewelry etc); cigars, cigarettes, chewing tobacco, snuff; and candies.

Small portions of the family meals can be given to them also (as often as possible), leave for a few hours, then dispose of it at the curb or the garbage, use your own discretion.

For Special Request: Add Gin, Beer or Palm Wine and their favorite foods and desserts.

NOTE: When cooking for Egungun do not add salt, it keeps the spirits away and they won't be around to hear your request.

Becoming spiritually in tuned with your altar will give you a sense of calm and completeness, because you are tapping into your Ancestral Soul. The Egungun will answer your questions or give you solutions in your dreams; keep a pen and paper close to your bed, and write down your first thoughts and dreams upon waking. And if you wake up with a craving it usually means that your Ancestors are requesting that food, especially if its something you don't regularly eat; like chitterlings and opossum; ha ha!!! Quickly prepare the meal or item and offer it to them, because, the Adimu (food offering of Love) may be requested to complete a task that you placed on them; or it could be to avert an upcoming problem that you are totally unaware of; use Adimu for special request, blessings, protection and/or strength. For an added treat play their favorite music loud, or if you play an instrument play and improvise (your spirit will soar). If you sing, belt one out, they will appreciate the attention and your singing voice will start to improve. True that!

You will find the customary way of worshipping your Egungun (Ancestors) to follow: There are several variations on this ancient ritual practice, and improvisation is allowed. When there are specific circumstances that occur in the family; you start by setting the tone by burning (one or a combination) herbs and keep it faithful. This list came from Tapping the Power Within by Iyanla VanZant a very handy book to have.

"Incense and Herbs Pleasing to Ancestral Forces and Spirits: Rosemary-to Invoke Spirits of Good Character (Iwa Pele); Lavender-Love and Peace; Cinnamon-Bring Good Luck, Aids in Powerful Meditation; Rose Buds-Attract Affection, Love and Peace; Sandalwood-Powerful Healing, Aids in

Clairvoyant Abilities; Sage-Purification and Wisdom; Anise Seed-Increase Communications and Intuitiveness; Jasmine-Attract Good Spirits and Love; Lemon-Aids in calling the Spirits for Protection; Verbena-Removes Curses placed on Family and You."

Customary Ceremony which is still practiced today is bequeathed to us from our Ancient African Ancestors, with a few updates. Priest/Priestess today use similar prayers for their Rituals and Libation Ceremonies.

1. Omi Tutu (cool water)

    Omi tutu Relatives

    Omi tutu Home

    Omi tutu Road

    Omi tutu Owner of Talkativeness

    Omi tutu Egungun (Ancestors)

    Death is no more

    Sickness is no more

    Tragedy is no more

    Loss is no more

    Obstacles are no more

    Unforeseen Evil is no more

    To be overwhelmed is no more

    The Immortality of our Fathers and Mothers

2. I salute Olodumare (God)

    I salute Orisha (Saints, Deity, and Essences of God)

    I salute all the Fathers of Orisha,

    I salute all the Mothers of Orisha, who are citizens of heaven

    Homage to the Sun, Moon, World and the Home

Homage to the Chief Babalawo (Ifa Priest)

3. I salute all Egungun (Ancestors) of my blood line who bow at the feet of Olodumare (God); Chief of the Heavenly World.

4. Egungun on my Fathers side;

5. SAY THIS PHRASE WITH EACH NAME YOU HAVE:

Mojuba (I pay respect) ___Their Name_____ Iba ye (Respect is paid): Mojuba Eddie Albert Ibaye; Mojuba Lola Mae Lightfoot Ibaye; Mojuba Robert L. Albert Ibaye; Mojuba Marqesha JoVann Albert Ibaye; Mojuba Marzamien Albert Ibaye; Mojuba Doll Albert Ibaye; Mojuba Jack Albert Ibaye; Mojuba Inez Lightfoot-Sherer-Smiley Ibaye; Mojuba Duke Smiley Ibaye; Mojuba Irene Lightfoot Ibaye; Mojuba Bertha Lightfoot Ibaye; Mojuba Corrine Palmore Ibaye; Mojuba Eddie Parks Ibaye; Mojuba Nathaniel Palmore Ibaye; Mojuba Roberta Stewart-Rembert Ibaye; Mojuba Amelia Thomas Ibaye; Mojuba Dan Palmore Ibaye; Mojuba Willie Wright Ibaye; Mojuba Roosevelt Wright Ibaye; Mojuba Frank Wright Ibaye; Mojuba Elmore Wright Ibaye; Mojuba Martina Palmore Ibaye; Mojuba Lucy Turner Ibaye; Mojuba Marcella Allen Ibaye; Mojuba Elizabeth Palmore Ibaye; Mojuba Ola Palmore Ibaye; Mojuba Michelle Eaton-Gray Ibaye; Mojuba Mose Wright Ibaye; Mojuba Blackfoot and Choctaw Ancestors Ibaye; Mojuba Middle Passage Ancestors Ibaye.

6. Egungun on my Mothers side; SAY THIS PHRASE WITH EACH NAME YOU HAVE:

Mojuba (I pay respect) ___Their Name_____ Iba ye (Respect is paid): Mojuba Walter Thomas Ibaye; Mojuba Anna Lee Robinson-Thomas Ibaye; Mojuba Richard Robinson Ibaye; Mojuba William Thomas Ibaye; Mojuba Caleb Robinson Ibaye; Mojuba Susie Thomas Ibaye; Mojuba Jim Thomas Ibaye; Mojuba Mary Ann Thomas-Vann-Brown Ibaye; Mojuba Monie Robinson Ibaye; Mojuba Major Robinson Ibaye; Mojuba Shelly Robinson Ibaye; Mojuba Sally Thomas Ibaye; Mojuba Amanda Thomas

Ibaye; Mojuba Edmund Thomas Ibaye; Mojuba Goddess Claren-cetta Brown Ibaye; Mojuba Tomi Shaw Ibaye; Mojuba John Rix-ter Ibaye; Mojuba Elijah Grover Ibaye; Mojuba Eloise Thomas Ibaye; Mojuba Mary Belle Robinson-Grover Ibaye; Mojuba Ruth Thomas-Snoten Ibaye; Mojuba Erman Vann Ibaye; Mojuba Lugary Thomas Ibaye; Mojuba Jefferson Grover Ibaye; Mojuba Alberta Thomas-Penneywell Ibaye; Mojuba Elijah Grover Ibaye; Mojuba Maddie Grover Ibaye; Mojuba Luverta Vann Ibaye; Mojuba Sylevester Vann Ibaye; Mojuba Mamie Vann Ibaye; Mojuba Jamie Vann Ibaye; Mojuba Gertrude Robinson Ibaye; Mojuba Isaac Grover Ibaye; Mojuba Choctaw and Blackfoot Ancestors Ibaye; Mojuba Middle Passage Ancestors Ibaye.

7. I pay Homage and respect to the Ancestors whose names have been forgotten.

I pay Homage and respect to the Ancestors of the Middle Passage and all who were extripated, hijacked, and uprooted from home.

I pay Homage and respect to the Ancestors that came and left so abruptly through Stillbirth, SIDS, Abortions, Racism, and Mal-practice, Pre mature Death and Miscarriages or Abiku (Infant that passes away shortly after their birth).

8. Kin Ka Ma Se (Let nothing happen to: _____Their Name_____; Here you would say the names of your living Family members, Friends, Relatives, Children, In-Laws, God Children and your Descendants.

ASE (So Be It)

NOTE: We are looking for any memorabilia of Our Ancestors named above. Also; if you have pictures and more names to add to our Egungun Ceremony, by all means make a copy and forward them it us. Very Important; If any of the names sound familiar to you we may be related (Please I just need information; remember at the beginning of this story IT CAME FROM OUR EGUN-

GUN; That means they want to be included in our rituals). Use the E-mail or snail mail at the end of the book. Thank You!!!

DATES AND EVENTS OF INTEREST IN OUR BLACK AFRICAN HISTORY

The names and events to follow can be called at Public Libation Ceremonies, to enhance the gathering as well as Formal Family gatherings if appropriate. No, we did not passively accept being hijacked, as you will see, but we were given up by some of our people in authority; the condemnation is still placed accurately where it belongs.

The following information was gleaned from Historical and Cultural Atlas ... by Asante & Mattson; as well as Shattering the Myths___ by Dr. Paul L. Hamilton and other publications such as older Funk & Wagnall and cited works.

36,000–4,500 BC Heru-khuti (Horus of the Two Horizons); The Great Sphinx approx. age

4,236 BC The 12 months of 30 days each and 5 days dedicated to the gods was developed by Kemet people and the original leap year added a year every 1,460 years.

2,980 BC Imhotep; Father of Medicine Father of Step Pyramids and their Architect; a Multi-genius

2,600 BC Pharaoh Djoser; Builder of the Step Pyramids

1491–1458 BC Queen Hatshesut of Egypt ruled as the King; First Female Pharaoh and created Peace and Prosperity for all.

1356–1339 BC 18th Dynasty Amenhotep IV; Introduced a religious revolution by declaring that there was only one aspect of God: Ra-Herakhty.

1403–1365 BC 18th Dynasty Queen Tiye Mother of Akhenaten and Tutankamen and wife of AmenhotepIII

500 BC Aesop An African slave in Greece that became famous for his Fables; Aesop's Fables were plagiarized and stolen by Socrates, Aristotle, Cicero, Julius Caesar and Shakespeare to name a few.

359–328 BC Clitus the Black Commander of Alexander the Greats Calvery and Governor of Bactria because of his fame was murdered by Alexander the Great in Libyan.

271–229 BC General Hamilcar Barcas Father of Hannibal, Carthaginian and "Lion's Brood"

247–183 BC Black Hannibal (the greatest General of all time); Carthaginian

238–148 BC King Massinissa of Namibia conquered Hannibal at Zamia and established Roman Empire

185–159 BC Terence a Poet, wrote six comedies, mastered Latin, Greek and Roman and is still revered in France and Italy.

69–30 BC Queen Cleopatra VII of Egypt became Co-Ruler of Rome With Caesar

145–211 AD Lucius Septimius Severus

189 AD Pope St. Victor I; Fought for Easter to be celebrated on Sunday.

193–211 AD Lucius Septimius Severus the Black Emperor of the World; Emperor of Rome and portrayed as 'white' an African born in Leptis Magna.

267–272 AD Queen Zenobia Great Warrior; Rome feared her power. She wrote an epitome of Oriental History.

313 AD Constantine 1 'white guy' Began converting and rewriting Christian doctrine.

354–430 AD St. Augustine African Bishop (Algeria), used the Church to reclaim African Ancestors portrayed as 'white' known as the "African man of Law" Orator Canonized and Proclaimed Doctor (Dr. of Church, Grace and Charity).

325–4th Century AD Yoruba people begin to travel West to West African forest belt to settle.

500–600 AD Chiefs and Kings emerge among the Yoruba due to new settlements.

1200–12th Century AD Ifamas gives birth to Christmas.

1300–1312 AD Al-Omari sent ships across the Atlantic for fishing and exploring; they landed in what is now known as Mexico.

1400–Present AD All those Africans that first invented, discovered, and initiated those innumerable items that were recorded under their Masters name and/or the company they worked for.

1645 AD First American bound slave ship (Rainbowe).

1663 AD First Major African revolt Gloucester, Va.

1735–1807 AD Prince Hall, Abolitionist and Organized the first African American lodge, Masonic leader, and the first interstate organization of and for Blacks in America.

1770 AD Crispus Attucks, First to die fighting against the British during American Revolution at "Boston Massacre"

1779 AD Baptist church in Savannah, Ga established by "Free Africans"

1779 AD First Independent Black denomination of the African Methodist Episcopal Church AMEC, founded by Richard Allen

1787 AD NW Ordinance prohibits slavery in NW Territories.

1787 AD Constitution approved to extend slavery for 20 years.

1800 AD Africans in Philadelphia petitioned Congress to end slavery.

1800 AD Gabriel Prosser organized the first large scale slave conspiracy in Virginia

1802 AD Alexander Dumas, pere Novelist wrote Three Musketeers, The Count of Monte Cristo to name a few.

1803 AD Toussaint L' Ouverture defeated Napoleon to free Haiti from slavery.

1804 AD Ohio enacts "Black Laws" preventing the movements of Africans.

1736–1806 AD Benjamin Banneker Astronomer and Mathematician, Surveyed and laid out Washington D.C. Produced first Almanac

1811 AD Paul Cuffe Entrepreneur owned a shipyard and sailed his own ships. He refused to pay taxes in Massachusetts until free Africans could vote.

1811 AD African, Slave Revolt in Louisiana.

1822 AD Denmark Vesey leads African revolt Charleston, South Carolina.

1760–1831 AD Bishop Richard Allen Called the Father of the Negro and First Black Bishop, Minister and Protest Leader.

1831 AD Nat Turner leads African revolt South Hampton, Va.

1834 AD Henry Blair First African to receive patent for invention of the Corn Planter and others.

1839 AD Cinque Leads African revolt aboard ship, flee to Cuba (Amistad).

1840 AD Peter S. Williams the New York Episcopalian priest declared "We are natives of this country; we only ask that we be treated as well as foreigners. Not a few of our fathers suffered and bled to purchase its' independence; we only ask to be treated as well as those who fought against it".

1841 AD Africans Revolt aboard ship and flee to Bahamas (Creole).

1844–1928 AD Elijah Mc Coy invented the lubricating device for Railroad cars called journal box

1850 AD $40,000 reward to catch Harriet Tubman the Conductor of the Underground Railroad

1852 AD Martin R. Delany Editor, Physician and Abolitionist Published the first full-length statement on Black Nationalism in America

1852–1889 AD Jan Ernst Matzeliger perfected the shoelasting machine

1856–1910 AD Granville T. Woods invented Railway communication system

1857 AD Dred Scott court case ruled against an African suing for his freedom. On grounds that his masters residence was in free Illinois territory, which entitled him to be released from bondage; Chief Justice Roger B. Taney noted, "… that Black men possessed no rights that white men were bound to respect …"

1858–1931 AD Daniel Hale Williams first Heart surgeon

1/1/1863 AD Emancipation Proclamation issued by President Lincolin only after the Union soldiers lost several battles; this Declaration really was a temporary measure to enlist "liberated" slaves so they could fight.

1865 AD Thirteenth Amendment abolishes slavery. (But read it!!)

1868 AD Fourteenth Amendment ratified African Civil Rights and extended citizenship rights, tied to vote. DVD the Corporation Parts 1&2 to see how it is being used today.

1869–1901 AD Twenty-Two Negros were elected to Congress of the United States. Two from Mississippi; Hiram R. Revels 1822–1901 AD and Blanche K. Bruce, served in the Senate 1841–1897 AD

1870 AD Fifteenth Amendment ratified the right to vote.

1874–1936 AD Maude Cuney Hare sang at the World famous opera house La Scala in Milan, Italy

1878 AD Lewis Latimer invents incandescent electric light.

1883 AD Sojourner Truth Civil Rights
A spokeswoman passes.

1892 AD Ida B. Wells Campaigns against Lynching

1817–1895 AD Frederick Douglass The Father of the Civil Rights Movement, Abolitionist, Editor, Author, and, Lecturer.

1896 AD a famous painting was purchased by the French Government for permanent display by Henry Ossawa Tanner (1859–1937) "The Resurrection of Lazarus"

1900 AD Egyptologist wrote Queen Nefertari and Queen Hatshepsut were not Ethiopians but Libyans who were counted as 'white'.

1901–1960 AD Zora Neale Hurston Anthropologist and Author studied the folk Culture of Blacks

1909 AD Matthew Henson First man to discover and set foot on the North Pole

1910 AD W.E.B. DuBois helped to found NAACP, National Association for the Advancement of Colored People and the Pan-African Movement. He stated "… We claim for ourselves every single right that belongs to a freeborn American, political, civil, and social; and until we get these rights we will never cease to protest and assail the ears of America"

1910 AD Jack Johnson becomes Boxing Heavyweight champ of the World, and remained a target by white society for his lifetime. Became the symbol of Black defiance

1911–1917 AD At the beginning of World War 1 the National Urban League organized to aid Blacks with their migration to the North. During that time more than 365 Negros were lynched in this country.

1919 AD 83+ African Americans lynched during "Red Summer of Hate" as KKK holds 200 public meetings.

1920 AD Marcus Garvey convenes the International gathering of Africans in Harlem under the Universal Negro Improvement Association and African Communities League.

1921–1971 AD Whitney M. Young, Founder of Urban League.

1923 AD George Washington Carver, Receives; the Spingarn Medal for Research.

1923 AD Garrett A. Morgan, Invents the Traffic Light.

1856–1931 AD Daniel Hale Williams Surgeon and Educator; performed the First Successful Operation on the Human Heart at Chicago Provident Hospital in 1893 AD.

1931 AD Elijah Muhammad Founder of the Nation of Islam

1932–1973 AD More than 400 Black Alabama sharecroppers and day labors were GIVEN Syphilis without their knowledge and simply studied by the Dept. of Health to gather information on the effects of the disease on the Untreated.

1935 AD Mary McLeod Bethune Forms the National Council of Negro Women; and Bethune-Cook College. Mary Bethune was the first Black women to receive major federal appointments.

1936 AD Jesse Owens; Wins Four Gold Medals in Berlin Olympics in front of Hitler; Track and Field. This upset the cr__ out of Hitler.

1937 AD Joe Louis Becomes Boxing Heavyweight Champion of the World; and held the title the longest.

1871–1938 AD James Weldon Johnson Civil Rights leader, Poet, Diplomat, 1920–1931 AD he served as the Executive Sec. of the NAACP, and Authored "Lift Every Voice and Sing", which became the Negro/Black National Anthem.

1870–1940 AD Robert S. Abbott Editor and Publisher of the Chicago Defender

1887–1940 AD Marcus Garvey Orator and Black Nationalist organized the first Black American Mass Movement of African Independence

1883–1941 AD Ernest E. Just Scientist, Zoologist and Professor at Howard U., contributed to the field of Embryology.

1940 AD Richard Wright Published Native Son

1940 AD Benjamin O. Davis, Sr. First African American Army General

1941 AD Dr. Charles Drew Develops Technique to separate properties of whole blood and preserve them for future uses. Later dies from the lack of his own invention; 1. Because he was Black; 2. There were no hospitals that would accept a Black man for treatment.

1945 AD John Johnson Established Ebony Magazine.

1948 AD Asa Phillip Randolph President of the Brotherhood of Sleeping Car Porters picketed outside the Democratic National Convention in Philadelphia demanding equal rights for all Negros

1875–1950 AD Carter G. Woodson organized the first Negro History Week; founded the Association for the Study of African American Life and History; called the Father of Black History.

1950 AD Ralph J. Bunche Political Scientist and Diplomat First Black to win Nobel Peace Prize for negotiating an end to first Arab-Israeli conflict

1955 AD Emmett Till (age 14); Kidnapped, Beaten and Lynched in Mississippi; being falsely accused by whites.

1956 AD Robert L. Albert Publisher the first Black Community Newspaper in Seattle, Wash. The Puget Sound Observer
He also recruited many young Blackman from the south to come out West and gain experience in the Forestry Service and gain career

opportunities with the Federal Government. He was very successful (This was when few of us worked for the Feds in any capacity.) He got plenty of flak for it!!!

1957 AD Martin Luther King, Jr. Organized the Southern Christian Leadership Conference (SCLC). Civil Rights leader and the major leader of the Freedom Movement of the 60's

1957 & 1958 AD Althea Gibson Top ranking Tennis Champion, won singles and doubles titles at Wimbledon

1908–1960 AD Richard Wright Author of Native Son and others; died in Paris, due to the increased hostility in America against Blacks.

1963 AD Medgar Evers Assassinated

1965 AD Malcolm X Assassinated in Harlem; Protest leader and Black Muslim minister; promoted strong alliances between Africans and African Americans

1965 AD Uprising in Watts, California Kills 35+ African Americans.

1966 AD Huey P. Newton and Bobby Seale Co-Founded the Black Panther Party in Oakland, Ca.

1966 AD Stokely Carmichael Elected head of the Student Nonviolent Coordinating Committee (SNCC)

1967 AD Thurgood Marshall Appointed to the Supreme Court.

1968 AD Martin Luther King Jr. Assassinated in Memphis, Tennessee

1908–1972 AD Adam Clayton Powell Jr. Politician and minister; the First Black Congressman from the East; the First Black chairman of a major congressional committee.

1975 AD Arthur Ashe Wins Wimbledon Tennis Championship in London, England

1889–1979 AD A. Philip Randolph Activist and Labor leader and founded the March on Washington movement; Co-Organized the

Brotherhood of Sleeping Car Porters. (10,000 Men Named George DVD)

1894–1984 AD Banjamin E. Mayes College president, Minister, and leader of World Council of Churches

1989 AD Ron H. Brown Elected Chairman of the Democratic National Committee and Later Assassinated.
There are many many more of our famous, which deserve our remembrances.

2003 AD Kendra S. James 20 year old Mother of 3 Murdered by police in Portland, Oregon

2005 AD Shirley Chisom passed First African American Women elected to Congress 1968–1982

2005 AD Marqesha J. Albert and Marzamien Albert her unborn son were Murdered by the racial profiling and discriminatory practices of the AMA and of the ER rooms and MD's of Seattle, Washington

HOW COULD THEY POSSIBLY PAY ENOUGH REPARATIONS? DO NOT LET THESE SKALLYWAGGES PASS LAWS SAYING WE NEED ACTUAL SLAVES BEFORE THERE IS A VALID CLAIM FOR REPARATION!!! WHAT! WHAT!
SOUNDS LIKE A GUILTY VERDICT TO ME

WISDOM

Wisdom is the finest beauty of a person.
Money does not prevent you from becoming blind.
Money does not prevent you from becoming mad.
Money does not prevent you from becoming lame.
You may be ill in any part of your body,

So it is better for you to go and think

Again and to select wisdom

Come and Sacrifice, that you may have

Rest in your body, inside and outside.

—Yoruba, Nigeria

WHAT WAS MY EGUNGUN PREPARING US FOR? THE WISDOM OF OUR EGUNGUN (ANCESTORS)!

At the time I started loosing sleep and trying to figure out what the dreams meant, I had no idea that they were actually preparing me and my family for a very devastating event.

The death by murder; of my only daughter and my first grandson was at the hands of doctors and hospital persons that viewed them through racial profiling eyes. I sought out attorneys and activist people that I thought gave a crap when injustice occurred, they don't. So I wrote a press release to get some assistance from I don't care where, they don't give a crap either.

The press release that I submitted is to follow:

PRESS RELEASE
FROM: TM ACADEMY FOR JUSTICE AND AFRICAN
SPIRITUAL CENTRE ©
8316 N. Lombard St., Ste#429
Portland, Oregon 97203

TO: THOSE CONCERNED;

Two more Murders occurred most recently as a result of Racial Profiling, Dereliction of Duty, Racism, Disrespect, Neglect, Malpractice, Discrimination and Social Injustice.

This time the police were not involved (not to let them off the hook), but another institution that we are suppose to trust; the hospital emergency rooms and doctors, the medical professionals. The medical professions are the progenitors of practice and experimentation on valuable human beings. Stop the charade!

Recently, our beautiful 22 year old, Roosevelt H.S. graduate, trusting, generous, intelligent, compassionate, creative, hard working (two jobs and no health coverage), drug free, AA degree carrying African American young women went to the emergency room in Seattle, WA, Aug. 10, 05; for the third time due to the pain and distress she was having, she was 5 ½ months pregnant.

Neither Marqesha Albert-Richmond nor her baby boy Marzamien survived. What did the professional do? Not much, not even their jobs. She and her fiancé waited for hours and were sent home with feeble instructions (put a pillow between your legs and put your feet up), and if that doesn't work return to the ER in 3 days. She presented with these symptoms i.e. headaches, spotting, cramping, swelling in her legs and feet; that should have raised flags in the dumbest intern.

You see they didn't bother to do the minimal normal test you perform on any and all pregnant women; especially in the hospital, (collect any and all fluids and run test!). If they were too busy, why wasn't she admitted? After all that was not the first time she had complained to these very same hospital and doctors earlier!

They only saw a single Black Female, pregnant, in pain, looking tired from lack of sleep, irritable from a long painful wait and dehydrated; I'm sure they thought if we wait long enough maybe they will leave, or she must be here for drugs or some other stereotype, racial profiling scenario, she can not be here for an illness due to complications of pregnancy.

Two days not four days after they sent them home, to put her feet up and place a pillow between her legs, SHE DIED and so did HER SON!!!!! They found her in that position. This was my DAUGHTER and GRANDSON.

Marqesha wanted to be a Mommy, and named her son Marzamien. We are so heart broken and are still in disbelief, it's so hard to breathe (do you know what I mean?!!). We miss our Daughter, Sister, Granddaughter, Niece, Auntie, Cousin, Goddaughter, Friend, Confidant and Mother-To-Be. I wish this PAIN on no one.

We have had a very prominent law firm way out of state look into this situation but due to the laws of Washington State and the staff needed to be dedicated to this case, the law firm would have to relocate to Washington to keep ahead of the cover ups occurring, it will be extremely difficult and expensive to try this case. I can hear the shuffle of papers and the shredding of documents as I write. On several occasions the lawyers requested documents and when they (hospital and doctor) responded there were obvious gaps and missing information forwarded to them, the "professionals" are working over time to cover each others behinds and get their story straight.

The Medical Examiner was constantly calling me to see if there were any latent conditions that could have caused this tragedy, there were none. The Medical Examiner took months to make his determination because of the lack of cooperation from the same sources. He was quite baffled and it took him some time before he was able to come to a cause. "If lab work was done they should have picked up on this ..." We were pleased that he took his time and so through.

Our family is now accepting tax deductible donations, to mount and fund a strong defense to win and change some laws. Is justice only for those that can afford it? And to use the donations received at the TMAJ&ASC in her name, to assist those young Black Women, Men and Families with advocacy assistance to help navigate through the barriers and document encounters, when and where they are needed and there will be an annual scholarship for a high school graduate from her High school. Plans for a Museum of African Culture. And to make these racist institutions change their policies (spoken or unspoken), to change and remove laws that state parents of adult children can not sue the pants off of the perpetrators on behalf of their children; Are You Kidding!!!! I dare them be-little parents (that's right you only use us when it's convenient for you) and further reduce our ability to protect our children.

T.M. Academy for Justice and African Spiritual Centre© (TMAJ&ASC), is a faith-based non profit organization that will accept on behalf of the family, tax deductible donations to hire and excellent law firm (if any of you want to be considered, to do what's right) and law makers that understand fully the dilemmas we are facing. Please submit information, request, interest, and donations to: TMAJ&ASC; 8316 N. Lombard St. Ste. #429; Portland, Oregon 97203

Or tmacademyjustice@aol.com HELP!

The goal is not another Black Child (regardless of age, that's your child), or family, suffers neglect or death at the hands of another racist institution, without them doing everything they can to prevent it, and us not having recourse. Protect the rights of the family, and to make this society understand we are not portrayed honestly, or respectfully and this must change. Our story is one of many! I am sad to say.

Thank You from:

Michele Albert, Family and Friends

4/2006

LET US BEHAVE GENTLY

Let us behave gently
  that we may die peacefully;
    That our children may stretch out their
      Hands upon us in burial

—Yoruba, Nigeria

God is greater than
All the Wizards and
Sorcerers on Earth

—Zulu Proverb

-Traditional African Proverbs-

CITED WORKS AND RECOMMENDED READINGS

Afrocentricity; Molefi Kete Asante 1991: African World Press

Ifa: An Exposition of Ifa Literary Corpus; Abimbola, Wande; 1997: Athelia Henrietta Press

Historical and Cultural Atlas; Asante, Molefik & Mark T. Mattson; 1992: MacMillan Pub.

The Movie: Angelique Kidjo World Music Portraits 2000

Ifa Divination: Communication Between, Gods and Men in West Africa; Bascom, William; 1969: Indian University Press

Egungun among the Oyo Yoruba S. O. Babayemi 1980: Board Publication Limited, Ibadan

Behold a Pale Horse; Cooper, Milton William; 1991: Light Technology Pub.

The Movie: Miss Evers' Boys

Santeria Garments and Altars; Speaking without a Voice; Ysamur Flores-Pena and Roberta J. Evanchuk 1994: University Press of Mississippi

The Movie: Spook that sat by the Door 1973

The OSHA Secrets of the Yoruba-Lucumi-Santeria Religion in the United States and the Americas; Cortez-Garcia, Julio; 2000: Athelia Henrietta Press

American Voudou Journey into a Hidden World; Davis, Rod; 1998: University North Texas Press

The Movie: Amistad

The Husia: Sacred Wisdom of Ancient Egypt; Maulana Karenga 1989: University of Sankore Press

The Movie: Buffalo Soldiers 1997

The Spirituality of African Peoples; Peter J. Paris 1995: Fortress Press

The Movie: Glory

The Movie: Roots

The Cultural Unity of Black Africa; Diop, Anta Cheikh; 1987: Third World Press

The Movie 10,000 Men named George

The Movie: Intruder 1961

Angels Don't Play This HAARP; Dr. Nick Begich 1995: Earthpulse Press

Selected Lectures on the Gosho; Daisaku Ikeda 1979: Nichiren Shoshu International Center

The Movie Dune

Black Skin, White Masks; Fanon, Frantz; 1967: Grove Evergreen Pub.

The Movie: Paul Robeson: Here I Stand 1999

A Journal of Native Consciousness; Griots; 1992: Griot Collective Larry, et al Abrams

The Redemption of Africa and Black Religion; St. Clair Drake 1991: Third World Press

Olodumare God in Yoruba Belief; Idowu, E. Bolaji; 1995: Original Publications

Ancestors Hidden Hands, Healing Spirits for your use and Empowerment; Ifagbemi, Min. Ra; 1999: Athelia Henrietta Press

Profiles in African Heritage; Jones, Edward L. 1979: African World Press

Yoruba Beliefs & Sacrificial Rites; J. Omosade Awolalu 1996: Athelia Henrietta Press

African Oracles in 10 Minutes; Kaser, R.T.; 1996: Avon Books

The Movie: Bowling for Columbine 2002

From The Browder Files; Anthony T. Browder 1993: The Institute of Karmic Guidance

The Movie: The Corporation Part 1&2

The Movie: Enron: The Smartest Guys in the Room 2004

Willie Lynch Letter the Making of a Slave; William Lynch and Kashif Malik Hassan-el 1999: Frontline Distribution International

Assertive Blacks … Puzzled Whites, Donald K. Cheeks, PhD, 1976, Impact Pub., Inc.

Orin Orisa: Songs for Selected Heads; Mason, John 1992: Yoruba Theological Archministry

The Yoruba World of Good and Evil; Mauge PhD, Conrad E 1994: House of Providence

The Movie: Rosewood

The Movie: Mississippi Burning

Introduction to Yoruba Philosophy, Religion and Literature; Ogunyemi, Yemi D. ; 1998

Creating Born Criminals; Rafter, Nicole Hahn; 1997: University of Illinois Press

Yoruba self-Help Using Adimu, Conrad E. Mauge Ph.D., 1997: House of Providence

The Movie: Deacons for Defense

Four New World Yoruba Rituals, John Mason 1993: Yoruba Theological Archministry

The Movie: Posse

The Debt: What America Owes to Blacks; Robinson, Randall 2000: Plume Press

The Movie: Amandla! A Revolution in Four Part Harmony 2002

Tales of Ancestors and Orisha; Scott, Lionel F. 1994

The Movie: Rize 2005

The Movie: Freedomland 2006

Flash of the Spirit; Thompson, Robert Farris; 1983: First Vintage Books

An African Prayer Book; Tutu, Desmond 1995: Doubleday

African Presence in Early Europe; Van Sertima, Ivan; 1986: Transaction Publications

They Came Before Columbus; Van Sertima, Ivan; 1977: Random House Trade

The Isis Papers the Keys to Colors; Welsing-Cress, Frances; 1988: Third World Press

The Movie: Bush Family Fortunes: The Best Democracy Money Can Buy 2004

The Movie: The Last King Of Scotland

Kill them before they Grow! The misdiagnosis of African American Boys in America's Classrooms; Michael Porter; 1998

The Movie: Wag the Dog 1997

Black American Leaders; Young, Margaret B. 1969

The Movie: Daughters of the Dust

Tales of Yoruba Gods and Heroes; Courlander, Harold

Fundamentals of the Yoruba Religion; Chief FAMA 1997: Ile Orunmila Communications

The Yoruba of Southwestern Nigeria and Santeria in the Southeastern United States; James A. Bailey 1991: Godolphin House

Idana Fun Orisa: Cooking for Selected Heads; John Mason 1999: Yoruba Theological Archministry
Ritual, Power, Healing and Community; Some, Malidoma

Tapping the Power Within; VanZant, Iyanla 1992: Harlem River Press

Acts of Faith; VanZant, Iyanla
The Spirit of the Black Man and the Women that Love Them; VanZant, Iyanla

Kwanzaa; Cedric McClester 1990: Gumbs & Thomas

The Movie: The Siege

The Movie: Dark City

Websites & E-Mail: TheTalkingDrum.com; RootsandRooted.org;
Mailto:
Olaodunjoye@aol.com or
TMAcademyJustice@aol.com

PART OF THE INAUGURAL SPEECH

"… Our deepest fear is that we are inadequate. Our deepest fear is that we are powerful beyond measure. It is our light, not our darkness that frightens us. We ask ourselves, who am I to be brilliant, gorgeous, talented and fabulous? Actually, who are you not to be? You are a child of God. Your playing small doesn't serve the World. There's nothing enlightened about shrinking so that other people won't feel insecure around you. We were born to manifest the glory of God within us. It's not just some of us; it's in everyone. And as we let our own light shine, we unconsciously give other people permission to do the same. As we are liberated from our own fear, our presence automatically liberates others …"

Nelson Mandela, 1994

GLOSSARY

Abo Ru, May sacrifice be accepted

Abo ye May sacrifice preserve the life

Abo si se May sacrifice manifest

Abiku, Infants that pass away shortly after their birth; the deity of "born to die"

Adimu, Love offering and/or gift of food for Orisa or Egungun

Affinity Egungun, Those close to you of Good Character, that are not in your blood line that have passed

Agbigbo, Bird of the Vulture family; regarded as a treacherous and dangerous bird who acts as an agent of Iku (Death)

Agemo, Chameleon; Servant of Orisa Obatala

ASE, Power; So Be It! The Power to get things done

Babalawos, High Priest of Priest; Father in the Knowledge of the Divination system; His reward is being in the Service of Orunmila, Fathers of Ancient Wisdom

Diaspora, Any scattering of a people with a common origin, background, and beliefs

DNA, Deoxyribonucleic Acid; Essential component of all living matter; and a basic material in the Chromosomes of the cell nucleus; contains the genetic codes and transmits hereditary patterns

Ebo, A Sacrifice or offering specifically requested by Orisa or Egungun, usually disclosed during divination

Efun, Clay from the shores of West Africa

Egungun, Bones; Ancestral Spirits

Epe, a Curse

Esu, Elegba, Deity of Communication; the Mediator and Messenger

Esu Odara, Lord of Transformation

Eugenics, the science of improving the population by controlled breeding for desirable characteristics

Extirpate, to uproot, hijack; to pull or pluck up by the roots; to root out; to eradicate; to destroy totally; to exterminate

Griots, Oral Tradition specialist; teller and performer of proverbs, sayings, folktales, philosophy, songs, music, history, and who was sold to who; past down word of mouth from generation to generation; and storyteller.

Iba ba T' Orun, Homage to generations in Heaven

Iba ye, Respect is paid

Ibeji, Twins, multiple births; Orisa protective of the children; considered a blessing, a rare occurrence

Ifa, Truth; the Divination system given to human beings by Orunmila as a means of communication

Ikose w' aye, a step into the World; the first Ceremony 3–7 days after birth

Ile-Ife, "The House Widening"; Cradle of Yoruba Culture

Imori, "know the Head"; divination to know the Ancestor; Ceremony 3–7 months after birth

Iwa Pele, Good Character, must be the dominant feature of a person's life because it is pleasing to Olodumare (God); Inherent nature

Kin ka ma se, "Let nothing happen to: _____"

Kwanzaa, A unique holiday that pays tribute to the rich cultural roots of African Ancestry. Kwanzaa means "the first" in Kiswahili. Kwanzaa is observed from Dec. 26th through Jan. 1st. Kwanzaa was founder in 1966 by Dr. Maulana Karenga, a Black Studies professor who describes himself as a cultural nationalist. Kwanzaa is based on Nguzo Saba (seven principles). Umoja (Unity); Kujichagulia (Self-Determination); Ujima (Collective Work and Responsibility); Ujamaa (Cooperative Economics); Nia (Purpose); Kuumba (Creativity); and Imani (Faith).

Libation, The act of pouring liquid (Alcohol or cool water), and sprinkling, either, on the ground or on shrub; in the honor of a Deity or Ancestor

Mojuba, "I pay respect"

Oba, King in Yoruba

Obatala, Represents collectively and symbolically the male Ancestral powers; purity and whiteness of the white cloth (not white people)

Odu Ifa, 16 major and 256 minor coded systems of deities, which are functioning in our lives, which are discovered during divinations; and providing solutions

Ogbe SA, Odu Ifa which speaks of friends becoming enemies; the return of the Spirits to Earth when they reincarnate

Olmec, Nubian (Black) Kemetics, Black Africans that settled on various Continents

Olodumare, God, Supreme Creator

Omi Tutu, Cool Water considered one of the best offerings to Spirit, a cooling off

Oni Bode, Gate Keeper in Heaven

Opa Egun, Tapping stick or cane designated to call upon Egungun

Ori, Our personal guardian, symbol of free choice; inner head received in Heaven, after meeting with Oni bode; Destiny

Orisa, Essences of God, Deities, Saints and Spirits

Orisa-nla, Praise name for Obatala; Creation, Wisdom and Purity

Orunmila, Present when you chose your destiny in Heaven; Christ; Buddha; Mohammed

Osun, Protection; the Sentential, always alert; regarded as very important Deity by Ifa priest

Ozone, Pale blue gas [O3]; used as a bleaching agent; formed by electrical discharges in the atmosphere; strong odor

Regentrification, To systematically change laws, rules land use policies that govern a community; move the existing population out and move in the desirable population in with all the benefits and incentives needed to up grade and take over a neighborhood by the "good ole boys"

Reparations, The act of repairing; to repair what is done; to repair a wrong; satisfaction for injury of Mind, Body, and Spirit

RNA, Ribonucleic Acid; Essential component of cytoplasm of all living cells; composed of long chains of phosphate and ribose along with several bases bonded to the ribose; one form carries the genetic information needed for protein synthesis in the cell

Sankofa, "… go back and fetch it"; leave no one behind

Sovereignty, The state of being a sovereign; the supreme power in a state; supremacy; possessing supreme dominion

To', it is sealed; said after Prayers, like Amen

Xenophobia, Fear, hatred of strangers or foreigners

Yoruba, Nation of people located throughout the World; base Ile Ife

MO DUPE

Thank you

978-0-595-42279-1
0-595-42279-9

Printed in the United States
78354LV00005B/1-18